Photo by T. Charles Erickson

A scene from the Huntington Theatre Company
production of *Sonia Flew*.

SONIA FLEW

BY MELINDA LOPEZ

DRAMATISTS
PLAY SERVICE
INC.

2

ACKNOWLEDGMENTS

This play was written because Ilana Brownstein invited me to be part of a remarkable program, the Huntington Playwriting Fellows. I owe her so much. My fellow fellows — Ronan Noone, John Kuntz and Sinan Unel — made the play better. Most important, my guardian angel Nicky Martin made it sing. Thanks to the wonderful actors who have worked on the play and who have all made it stronger. Finally and most particularly, I want to acknowledge my parents, beloved husband Matthew, and Maddy — it's for you.

SONIA FLEW was originally produced by the Huntington Theatre Company (Nicholas Martin, Artistic Director; Michael Maso, Managing Director) in Boston, Massachusetts, opening on October 8, 2004. It was directed by Nicholas Martin; the set design was by Adam Stockhausen; the costume design was by Kristin Glans; the lighting design was by Frances Aronson; the sound design was by Drew Levy; the production stage manager was David H. Lurie; the stage manager was Jane Siebels; and the dramaturg was Ilana Brownstein. The cast was as follows:

SONIA/MARTA	Carmen Roman
DANIEL/TITO	Jeremiah Kissel
ZAK/JOSE	Ivan Quintanilla
JEN/YOUNG SONIA	Amelia Alvarez
SAM/ORFEO	Will LeBow
NINA/PILAR	Zabryna Guevara

CHARACTERS
All characters double as noted:

SONIA, 50s, mother, and MARTA, 60s, housekeeper

DANIEL, 50s, father, and TITO, neighbor

ZAK, 19, son, and JOSE, 19, young man

JEN, 17, daughter, and YOUNG SONIA, 15, daughter

SAM, 70s, grandfather, and ORFEO, 50s, father

NINA, 28, soldier, and PILAR, 35, mother

Note: All six actors play different characters in the first and second acts. Only PILAR and ZAK appear in both acts (excepting Act Two, Scene 5).

SETTING

The first act is set in Minneapolis, December 2001. The second act is set in Havana, April 1961.

A NOTE ON ACCENTS

In Act Two, please assume that the characters are speaking their native tongue, and through the magic of theatre we can understand them. Therefore — no accents.

Please overlap dialogue. Pace is very fast throughout.

SONIA FLEW

ACT ONE

Prologue

Pilar stands in the surf. She throws flowers.

PILAR. Calm the waters, Oshún. Lady of Charity, have mercy on me. Prepare my passage. Sand. And sea. Ninety miles spread across the ocean like oil on water. *(Sound of waves.)* I am not afraid. They say that only God can give life and only God can take it away. But they are men. And they have never given life. I have. Does this make me God? I have a daughter. *(Lights rise on Sonia, isolated.)* I have a daughter. I have a daughter. *(Pilar steps under the waves and disappears.)*
SONIA. And I said, I do not forgive you. I will never forgive you. You have broken my heart.

Scene 1

Minneapolis. Lights up on the dining area of the home. A table is half-set for a formal meal. Candles are prominently placed. A Christmas tree in the corner decorated with Star of David ornaments. Sonia is rummaging through kitchen cabinets, throwing Jell-O molds around.

SONIA. Jen!
JEN. *(Offstage.)* Mom!
SONIA. Jen!
JEN. *(Offstage.)* Homework!
SONIA. The pan?
JEN. *(Offstage.)* Chemistry.
SONIA. The pan! The pan, you know the one.
JEN. *(Offstage.)* Boyle's law!
SONIA. Gas expands to fill the space it occupies.
JEN. *(Offstage.)* In the cupboard by the thing!
SONIA. *(Looking.)* No!
JEN. *(Offstage.)* Mom!
SONIA. Your grandfather!
JEN. *(Entering.)* It's under the thing —
SONIA. Help me with this.
JEN. Mom, no one eats that 7-Up salad.
SONIA. It's tradition —
JEN. Lime Jell-O and 7-Up and cream cheese?
SONIA. Cottage cheese.
JEN. Ugh.
SONIA. And cherries — it needs this special pan. This is the only one — this mold, this —
JEN. Why is this so important?
SONIA. Because there are things in life — there are — rules. That develop. Over time. A way of doing things, that become, in time, important. In Wisconsin, if you showed up to a church supper and the Jell-O was in the wrong pan, well, it mattered. People let you know, in subtle ways — small helpings, what was left on the plate,

8

who got asked to dance —

JEN. Boys wouldn't dance with you because you used the wrong Jell-O mold?

SONIA. We're talking very codified behavior. Very …

JEN. Medieval.

SONIA. My point is, after a lifetime, you become, without thought, you become — a cog in the wheel — what is it?

JEN. Spoke.

SONIA. What?

JEN. Wheels don't have cogs, they have spokes.

SONIA. My point is I can't have Christmas without 7-Up salad,

JEN. Christmas is next week.

SONIA. A whole season of lights.

JEN. Hanukkah's over.

SONIA. And I can't have 7-Up in any old mold.

JEN. Mom, that's just weird. You're just a transplant. Why can't we codify mojitos, or something a little sexier?

SONIA. What do you know from sexier?

JEN. Why do you have to be so weird?

SONIA. I hope it snows on Christmas Eve.

JEN. It was better when we spent eight days of Hanukkah on Key Biscayne in a bikini.

SONIA. New traditions. Lox on white bread. Frijoles and a cheese log.

JEN. By the way, there's no 7-Up.

SONIA. Excuse me?!

JEN. I drank the last of it this afternoon.

SONIA. There's no 7-Up — I don't believe this — do I have to run the damn country too? I'm going out — could you please — I don't know — set the table or something — your grandfather comes in a few — keys, okay, wallet — ZAK!

ZAK. *(Offstage.)* I'm online —

SONIA. Your grandfather — airport — traffic —

ZAK. A minute —

SONIA. Now, please! Jen, put out the dreidel, you know your grandfather likes to see a dreidel —

JEN. No one plays dreidel — that's like for five-year-olds —

SONIA. If there's a tree, there's a dreidel. That's the deal. Zak? Please!

ZAK. Coming!

SONIA. Then why aren't you here? Jen — remember, sunset, it's very important that we're ready by sunset for the Sabbath —

JEN. I know, Mom.

SONIA. I want everything to go just right with your Papí's visit — he hasn't been up North in so long —

JEN. Why couldn't we go to Florida like we always do —

SONIA. A little yule log, a little rugelach — I'll be right back —

JEN. In Miami it's eighty-two.

SONIA. No planes.

ZAK. *(Entering.)* Mom?

SONIA. Zak. Sam — American — flight number two-fifty-some-thing — here's the info —

ZAK. It's up to eighty-four in Miami.

JEN. Mom!

SONIA. Jenny! Find the dreidel — where's the menorah? Find the menorah. Sam, menorah, candles, 7-Up. Jesus Lord give me strength —

ZAK. Mom — I need a minute with you —

SONIA. Is this about the Timberwolves? Because I'm not chang-ing my mind, Zak — this dinner is a big deal for your dad — foot-ball can wait —

ZAK. Oh my God, basketball-basketball-basketball —

SONIA. Isn't he hilarious when he gets all red like that?

ZAK. And no, it's about something else, and I need some time with you —

JEN. Don't.

SONIA. Later, later — *(She exits.)*

JEN. You can't tell her now. You can't possibly tell her now. She's wired.

ZAK. I told you.

JEN. I think it sucks

ZAK. No but really …

JEN. Sucks sucks sucks.

ZAK. Don't hold back.

JEN. What about school?

ZAK. I'm not ready.

JEN. You're ready for war but not school?

ZAK. It's hard to explain, but basically.

JEN. It's really done?

ZAK. Done.

JEN. It's for like, what, a few years?

ZAK. Five to start …

JEN. Five years?

ZAK. I'll come home …

JEN. In a body bag.

ZAK. I'll finish school then.

JEN. Mom is going to freak.

ZAK. I won't even get posted anywhere. It'll all be over already.

JEN. This sucks.

ZAK. Look, this guy came to talk to us —

JEN. A recruiter?

ZAK. A soldier, okay?

JEN. Nazis.

ZAK. And he just made me think a lot — I mean, we have it good over here, you know, and I wonder all the time, about — you know, who pays for this? I mean —

JEN. The guy with the medical degree, asshole.

ZAK. I don't mean Dad, asshole, I mean, who pays, you know? Who keeps it together? Who keeps us safe?

JEN. Zak.

ZAK. No, shut up — I'm not brainwashed. I give a shit. Don't you? Shouldn't we? What did we ever do for it? You and me, Jen, what did we do for it?

JEN. Are you on crack? Because you can't actually sign if you're on some kind of —

ZAK. It's my time, Sissy. It's my time. I can't sit around.

JEN. Just finish school.

ZAK. It's done.

JEN. Done?

ZAK. On Monday, it'll be done.

JEN. Monday?

ZAK. That's when I sign the contract.

JEN. Monday's Christmas Eve —

ZAK. I have to tell Mom. Do you think she'll be okay?

JEN. It has to be rescinded if you're not … *corpus delecti* or something.

ZAK. *Compos mentis,* dumb ass.

JEN. Don't do it.

ZAK. The Few. The Proud.

JEN. The Brainwashed.

ZAK. Help me with Mom.

JEN. She'll be okay. Mom's always okay. What about Dad?

ZAK. He knows.

JEN. Okay, she won't be okay about that.

ZAK. She'll be okay. Are you okay?

JEN. I think I really hate you right now.

ZAK. I'll be fine.

JEN. Not for you, for me! How am I going to stand living here without you?

ZAK. You've done okay so far.

JEN. Yeah, but Brown was someplace I could visit. Meet guys, drink beer. Now you're going to freaking Afghanistan or something.

ZAK. They're still burning, Jenny. The towers. I went, you know, and they're still burning.

SONIA. *(Sings offstage.)*
　　When the snow lay 'round about.
　　Deep and crisp and even.
Dammit!

JEN. Why does it have to be you?

SONIA. *(Reentering.)* Zak — what are you still doing here — I don't want Sam sitting at the airport — we have to make this go smoothly — it's a long trip for him —

ZAK. Mom. I have to —

SONIA. You know, I got down the driveway, and I thought, "What the hell am I doing? Jen is right." Oh-ho, stop the presses, I said it — Jen is right — I don't even like that salad. And so, my dear, in honor of you, we are starting a new tradition this year. A year without 7-Up salad. What do you think, my handsome son?

ZAK. I have to tell you something.

SONIA. What? What is it. Oh my God, what happened. Why are you looking like that? Jenny?

JEN. Go ahead, cowboy.

SONIA. Someone's pregnant? Someone's dead. Oh God, Zak, whatever it is, it's okay. Whatever it is. What is it? *(Lights fade. Sonia stands isolated.)* I always dreamed of snow. Awake, I couldn't make it out. Imagine it. But I would dream of this unknown thing — frozen water from the sky — at home — my first home in Cuba — we only had this hot rain, miserable, hot water, these torrential downpours — so regular you could set your watch by them. But in my dreams, snow was always clean and cold, and when it reached your body, it shattered — tiny broken crystals that made a sound like music.

Of course when I finally saw snow, real snow, well that was Wisconsin, I arrived in April — and it was so ugly, so dirty. It was a terrible day that day, frigid, windy. And the snow was black. Just mounds of black, rotted ice. Well, I was. Disappointed. *(Light fades.)*

Scene 2

Sonia and Daniel setting the table for Shabbos —

DANIEL. What time is it?
SONIA. Have you spoken to him?
DANIEL. Yes.
SONIA. Well?
DANIEL. Give him some time. He's trying to find a way to —
SONIA. What?
DANIEL. Help — I don't know.
SONIA. College can't help? Medical school, law school can't help?
DANIEL. He's almost nineteen.
SONIA. Pass me those.
DANIEL. He hasn't signed anything.
SONIA. He told you that?
DANIEL. Yes. Where's the thingy?
SONIA. You're not even concerned?
DANIEL. Of course I am.
SONIA. Thingy. *(The thingy.)* Your father's late.
DANIEL. What time is it?
SONIA. We have time.
DANIEL. Don't do that, I hate it when you do that —
SONIA. Get a watch —
DANIEL. Let me see *(He reaches for her arm.)* —
SONIA. It's quarter-past, okay?
DANIEL. Is it?
SONIA. And thirty-one seconds. Thirty-two. Thirty-three, thirty-four —

DANIEL. Okay okay — the candles — the roast. You made the kugel?

SONIA. I would like to have had some time alone with Zak to talk, to reason with him —

DANIEL. What did you say?

SONIA. Nothing. I didn't say anything — I was just so ...

DANIEL. *Mi amor,* we'll find the time. Look, your eyes —

SONIA. What?

DANIEL. You're doing that thing, getting squinty —

SONIA. Oh God, Botox —

DANIEL. I love it. I love you. Kiss me.

SONIA. I can't, it's sixteen past, and eight seconds, nine, ten —

DANIEL. I'll go call.

SONIA. *(Calling upstairs.)* Jen, get offline!

JEN. *(Offstage.)* Mom!

DANIEL. *(Dialing.)* I'll use the cell —

SONIA. Get offline now —

JEN. *(Offstage.)* We need high speed already!

SONIA. Come help me with dinner —

JEN. *(Offstage.)* Grampa's here —

DANIEL. Hello, Dad? Where are you?

JEN. *(Entering.)* They just pulled in —

DANIEL. *(On the cell.)* They're pulling in —

SONIA. I know.

DANIEL. *(On the cell.)* Okay, Dad, we're all here. *(To Sonia.)* He's getting out of the car.

SONIA. Jen, get the porch lights.

JEN. It's not dark.

SONIA. Get the porch lights.

DANIEL. *(Still on the phone.)* No Dad, let Zak carry that — Dad, please — he wants to carry his own bag —

SONIA. So let him!

DANIEL. *(On the cell.)* Dad, please, let Zak —

SONIA. Daniel, hang up the phone and open the door, for goodness —

DANIEL. *(Opening the door.)* Dad — please let, Dad —

ZAK. *(Offstage.)* Don't worry, Grampa, I got it ...

SAM. I can carry my own ... not helpless *(Entering.)* ... I can't cross the street without someone jumping up to take my arm. Here, feel that. Now feel that, does that feel like seventy-five?

ZAK. Gramps, it feels like —

SAM. Watch it now ...

ZAK. Seventy —

SAM. There you go.

ZAK. — Four —

DANIEL. Pop, how was the trip?

SAM. Hey hey —

SONIA. *(To Jen.)* Go kiss your grandfather.

JEN. Mom.

SAM. And how is my jewel of the tropics?

SONIA. Sam — you're looking so well.

JEN. Papí. *(Kissing him.)*

SAM. Now I can die happy — surrounded by such pulchritude — How's my little daisy?

SONIA. Who's talking about dying?

JEN. Good Papí.

DANIEL. A drink for you, Dad?

SAM. Don't crowd me, you're crowding me —

ZAK. *(Carrying all the bags out.)* I'll take these upstairs.

SONIA. Your coat —

SAM. Youth! It's wasted on the young, did you ever hear that?

JEN. What did you bring me?

SAM. Grapefruit!

JEN. That's it?

SAM. Do you see that? In my day, it was seen and not heard.

JEN. When was that exactly?

SAM. Don't push me, young lady, you're not too old for me to give you a *potsch* in the *tuchus*. And for the lady of the house ... *(He produces a pastry box tied with a string.)*

SONIA. My God, not *pasteles!*

SAM. *Pasteles.*

SONIA. Oh Sam!

JEN. Open them open them!

SONIA. Hey hey hey! You got grapefruit —

JEN. Swap you —

SONIA. These are for tomorrow morning — divine at breakfast.

DANIEL. Jenny, offer your Papí something to drink.

SAM. Parched. Parched I am.

JEN. Hot or cold.

SAM. Fizzy.

DANIEL. Here, have a seat. Let me take these — long trip?

SAM. Flight was right on time, least they can do now — and they have these fancy-Dan seats, all upgrade, everything upgrade. If you live long enough you'll see your entire life upgraded — and that kid of yours drives like a demon —

SONIA. Zak?

SAM. Like his old man!

SONIA. Danny, you have to talk to him about that.

DANIEL. About that too?

SONIA. Who's having wine?

DANIEL. Time check —

SONIA. Get a watch.

SAM. Twelve minutes —

JEN. Till what?

SAM. Sunset — can I time an entrance or what?

JEN. Oh right, the candles.

SONIA. Jen — the food —

JEN. I'm not bringing out the roast.

SONIA. Jennifer!

JEN. Meat is murder. I'm making a tofu burger.

DANIEL. Did you know that two hundred thousand acres of rainforest are destroyed each week clearing land for soybeans?

JEN. That is not true.

DANIEL. NPR. Soy is the leading crop in Brazil. Ten million acres a year. Gone.

JEN. I hate you right now.

DANIEL. Bring out the roast.

SAM. Don't act like you never have Shabbos.

JEN. We never have Shabbos.

SONIA. Jen.

JEN. When we're with Papí, we have Shabbos.

SAM. And?

JEN. And a lovely Shabbos it is, too!

DANIEL. You just like to get the blessing —

SONIA. Jenny — kitchen —

JEN. I live to serve.

SONIA. *(Aside.)* Danny, is that true about the soy thing?

DANIEL. Shh …

SONIA. *(She mouths.)* I adore you.

ZAK. *(Entering.)* Your stuff's all set.

SAM. Thank you, Zakele. Danny can you believe this kid? Look at the shoulders on this kid!

ZAK. Come on, Grampa —

SAM. Put that boy in a uniform!

DANIEL. Dad.

SONIA. Sam, please.

ZAK. I told Grampa on the ride down.

SAM. I just wish his grandmother could see him.

SONIA. Anyone for wine?

SAM. Her family — all fighters over there —

SONIA. Or something harder?

DANIEL. Yes — to both —

JEN. In Israel?

SONIA. Well, I will then …

DANIEL. Zak hasn't made a final decision yet —

ZAK. Yes, I have.

SAM. I thought that's what he said —

ZAK. I have —

SONIA. Your father is just saying that we haven't had the chance to sit down and discuss this as a family —

ZAK. What's to discuss?

SONIA. It's crazy for you to go and make a decision like this without including us —

ZAK. Crazy?

DANIEL. Honey, now may not be the best time —

SONIA. I didn't bring it up —

DANIEL. Dad — we've got tickets for the ballgame if you're up for it —

JEN. Let's go upstairs, Zak.

ZAK. I've given it a lot of thought, it's not just some —

JEN. Zak, I found some excellent porn online —

DANIEL. She's joking, Dad —

ZAK. Half-baked idea —

SAM. I can tell you from my experience —

DANIEL. Dad —

SONIA. You act as if it's perfectly reasonable — look at him —

ZAK. Come on Mom —

SONIA. A's in the Ivies, hockey player, I mean he's a Fulbright just waiting to happen, and his social conscience — I mean what happened to the war on poverty — that — those groups that you —

why not the Peace Corps for God's sake, why do you have to use ammunition?

JEN. There was that guy from school who went into the Peace Corps and got malaria and died —

DANIEL. Not now —

JEN. I'm just saying —

ZAK. Because that's not how the world works.

SONIA. What do you know about how — the world works, listen to him, he sounds like he's been — like he's a grown, man, like an old man — What do you know about it? Nothing — Do you think that by following the orders of — of an impaired leader — do you think —

ZAK. That's not what I think —

SAM. Impaired? What does she mean impaired?

DANIEL. Don't bait her, Dad.

ZAK. And I don't think it's fair for you to make these kinds of assumptions about what I believe —

SAM. She must mean something by that.

DANIEL. You know what she means.

SONIA. Sam, I'm sorry. This is a matter for us — you know I had hoped we could have some family time to talk about it first.

SAM. Family time?

JEN. Excuse me —

ZAK. Grampa's happy for me. He did it, and he's happy for me.

SONIA. Filling your head with —

ZAK. With what?

SONIA. You never asked me. You never came to me. And your father. To. Even ask what we thought. How can you?

JEN. Umm, everyone?

DANIEL. Not now, Jennifer

SAM. I'm not family?

ZAK. You can tell it all to the recruiting officer, Mom. Tell him how you carry your running shoes in the trunk of the car in case the roads get blown out —

SONIA. I carry snow boots, too — in case the battery dies — I suppose you think that means something —

ZAK. Tell the recruiter that you don't fly anymore.

SONIA. That was a one-time thing — the doctor said it was stress-related —

DANIEL. Come on, Zak, your mom is doing much better —

ZAK. They had to bring the plane back to the gate! They had to turn the plane around because of her —

SONIA. You weren't there!

ZAK. You won't get on a plane, Mom. That's why Grampa came to us this year. Why doesn't anyone just say that? What's next?

SONIA. A lot of people won't fly now.

ZAK. I did. Grampa did.

SONIA. Why are you doing this?

ZAK. Why are you? I have never seen you back off from anything in my life — you taught me that — fight back, right? Isn't that what you taught us? You were never afraid of anything. And now all of a sudden …

SONIA. Oh honestly!

ZAK. I see when you turn on the news in the morning, you're waiting to hear which city it was this time —

SONIA. That's not so!

ZAK. It is so! It is, because I know you and because you're no different from me, and that's how I am. I see — your lip does this thing — it gets tense there before you hear the top story, and if it's only another school shooting, or a CEO in jail, then that's good news. Because it gives us all another day to wait it out — I know that's true because that's what I do. And I'm sick of waiting. I'm sick of waiting for some towel-head to give us ours —

SONIA. Danny?

DANIEL. There's no need for that.

ZAK. So you go see the recruiter, and you tell him that this is all okay, sitting around, and wondering if tomorrow is the day — Tell him that you're not planning to do anything about it.

JEN. Excuse me, everyone —

SONIA. You watch that, Zak — you watch that tone — I love this country. I made this country mine — I wasn't born into it — I had to make a vow — don't you go shoot off your slogans at me because I make it a better place every day —

ZAK. You do it your way at the public defender's office — I'll do it mine.

DANIEL. What is this? Cowboy justice?

ZAK. Forget it. I'm done. *(Beat.)*

JEN. It's dark. That's all.

SAM. Sunset.

JEN. The blessing.

SONIA. You have such a limited understanding of these things.
ZAK. Whatever.
SAM. Kids, huh?
DANIEL. Honey. Everyone. Let's. Dad came all this way. Let's eat. Let's, come on, Zak. We'll find time. Sonia. Please.
SONIA. Sure. Yes. The organic roast, free-range, vegetarian-fed, untouched by human hands. It smells great. I'm starving. Starving. *(She makes her way to the table.)*
JEN. Me too. Zak?
ZAK. Me too. Grampa?
JEN. Dad, is that true about the soy thing?
DANIEL. Absolutely. *(They are all standing at the table, except for Sonia, who is sitting and helping herself to more wine.)*
SAM. Daniel?
DANIEL. Honey? Sonia. We'd like to begin now.
SONIA. Pull up a chair.
DANIEL. Honey. The candles.
SONIA. Matches are over there.
DANIEL. Please don't do this, Sonia.
SONIA. What am I doing?
DANIEL. You need to light the candles, Sonia.
SONIA. Do I?
SAM. Danny, I can.
DANIEL. Sonia. The woman of the house lights the candles. We've done this before.
JEN. I can do it, Dad.
DANIEL. It is your mother's job. It's her job. Sam is here, Zak is here, we'd all like to sit and eat now. Please light the candles and give the blessing. Sonia. Sonia.
SONIA. Why is that exactly? Why does the woman do that?
DANIEL. What is happening to you?
JEN. I will, Mom, it's okay. What's the big deal?
SONIA. Don't interrupt!
SAM. The woman — the wife. The good wife is the beginning and the end. The alpha and omega. She is the life giver and life renewer. The rejuvenator. Home is a circle beginning and ending at the mother. She prays for peace and renewal and for twenty-four hours no work done. A day of rest. Peace.
DANIEL. Please light the candles.
SONIA. Peace for a day. That's really it? Twenty-four hours. And

then what?

ZAK. I don't know.

SONIA. You know, Zak, I've spent my life preparing for the moment when I find out you're dead. Brave is watching your kid ride a bike for the first time. Brave is your son's first sailboat — I have let you go a million times. You don't need to make the world safe for me.

ZAK. I'm swearing in Monday, Mom.

SONIA. Please, Zak. Don't go to war.

ZAK. I'm sorry. It's something I've decided.

DANIEL. Put it aside, Sonia. Tonight we celebrate what we have. Light the candles, bless the meal, bless the children. Sonia...?

SONIA. Light them yourself. *(They stand deadlocked. Jen takes the matches, lights the candles and begins the prayer.)*

JEN. *Baruch atah adonai elohenu melech haolam, asher kidshanu bemitzvotav vitzivanu le hadlik ner shel shabbat ...*

SAM. Amen. *(Lights fade. Sonia alone, isolated in a light.)*

SONIA. Children leaving. It was very loud. The soldiers were especially loud. The boots. And everywhere, there were families crying. Announcements on the speakers. Planes departing. I walked to the gate through a hallway of glass, and my family was looking in. Or they had said they would be, they said to look for them, but I was — I was only watching my shoes. I had on a new pair, my first pair of heels. But they rubbed my toes raw. The blister burned so much, it's all I could think about. I suppose I must have walked right by my parents. My father would have whistled for me, I suppose. He had a special whistle for me — but with all the noise I couldn't hear.

The planes. Silver, so beautiful. How could something that big ever fly?

Other things happened. I know they searched us, but I don't remember that. I lost my ring. Or did they take it? A pocketful of basil leaves. And then I was in the air. I asked to use the bathroom. A nice American girl showed where, and I took my shoes off there and threw them away. They hurt me. And they were Cuban shoes. It made sense to me then, although it was a terrible nuisance when I arrived in Miami. *(Fade lights.)*

Scene 3

Daniel and Sonia, alone. They stare at each other.

DANIEL. Something is wrong with you.

SONIA. Yes.

DANIEL. That you can do this. In my house. Our home.

SONIA. I don't know …

DANIEL. Something has happened to you. That you. My God, Sonia, my father.

SONIA. I know.

DANIEL. How could you dare. To him? Family? Bullshit, when he lost his entire — how do you dare? To me? Is there something that I? No — It can't be really, I can't think that there could be any way of understanding your. Behavior. Explain your behavior. I am listening.

SONIA. I can't.

DANIEL. I have always been, I think, a rational person. A sensitive person.

SONIA. Yes.

DANIEL. I thought you thought so.

SONIA. I do.

DANIEL. Whatever this is about, whatever — is it me? Have I not — ? To your guests? To your children? Your son?

SONIA. Why do you always take his side?

DANIEL. Whose side?

SONIA. Always. There is no … perspective. Whatever he wants. The golden boy, and what I want, say, what I want for him, for us, the family —

DANIEL. Zachary?

SONIA. Yes.

DANIEL. I am sure if you think about it, you'll see that this is not so. I do not side —

SONIA. Yes! It is so — it is so — always, you always —

DANIEL. There is nothing to be gained by attacking me on this.

SONIA. Don't counsel me, Daniel. I am not one of your patients.

Don't tell me how to frame my hurt. I know damn well I can say, "I feel hurt when you do this to me," but it's not what I mean. I am attacking you. Fine. You are attacked. Yes. You always take his side. I need you to hear this.

DANIEL. I am listening.

SONIA. I'm sorry.

DANIEL. Okay.

SONIA. I will not be counseled.

DANIEL. I hear you.

SONIA. Your son is throwing away his life.

DANIEL. I don't agree.

SONIA. He is. Daniel. He is. My son. It's not supposed to go this way. It's not supposed to be this way. No. I know, I know what you think before you even say it. I know.

DANIEL. That leaves me very few options, Sonia.

SONIA. Can't you speak with him?

DANIEL. I don't think I can change his mind, if that's what you mean.

SONIA. You think I'm crazy.

DANIEL. Why do you think that?

SONIA. Don't counsel me!

DANIEL. I'm not counseling! Do you think I would take this abuse from a patient?

SONIA. Do you think I'm crazy?

DANIEL. I'm not trained to think people are crazy.

SONIA. Do you think I'm crazy?

DANIEL. Yes, a little.

SONIA. Thank you.

DANIEL. Is this about Zachary?

SONIA. You think it's not?

DANIEL. I think this is about us. Not about Zak. It's about what you did in there. At this table on a holy night —

SONIA. Since when? Since because your father came? Since when are we so pious? I never agreed to that. I never agreed to — we've done it all your way for so long.

DANIEL. What is my way? You said, you told me religion was not something important to you — you gave me charge of their — you agreed — yes — You chose not to choose. It's not about a stupid dreidel.

SONIA. Why do we pretend for Sam? Why do you pretend for him?

DANIEL. Pretend? What are we pretending?

SONIA. The prayer. The blessing. The humility. Every year with the Sabbath, the candles, agreeing — agreeing, always yes.

DANIEL. It's not a pretense. It's about respect.

SONIA. Respect?

DANIEL. This is important to him. And so it is important to me. To us. His family. You are his family. You are his — yes.

SONIA. It's what children do.

DANIEL. Yes

SONIA. It's something that children do. *(Her breathing become labored — a panic attack.)* I'm having trouble here. I'm having trouble breathing here.

DANIEL. Let me get you something.

SONIA. No.

DANIEL. I'll get you something.

SONIA. I'm having trouble seeing here.

DANIEL. Sit down. Here — sit here.

SONIA. Danny.

DANIEL. Head down.

SONIA. Sit with me. *(She drops her head between her legs, and breathes.)*

DANIEL. You need to eat something.

SONIA. No. It feels good. The pain feels good. Just sit with me.

DANIEL. I'm here, baby. *(They sit quietly.)* How're you doin'?

SONIA. Can't talk.

DANIEL. I love you. Sonia. Breathe.

SONIA. Better.

DANIEL. Breathe.

SONIA. Better.

DANIEL. Is this what happened on the plane?

SONIA. Everything went black, and then I was burning up. Couldn't breathe. I guess I was crying. Moaning, they said.

DANIEL. That's what the stewardess said.

SONIA. I guess I was disturbing first class.

DANIEL. They said you threw a punch or two.

SONIA. I didn't want to be on that plane. I can't describe it. It was just a stupid conference. There wasn't any need for me to go to a stupid conference. They found a better speaker. Next time, it'll be fine.

DANIEL. It's too much, all the holidays. We try to cram in too much. Too many gods. Next year, we simplify.

SONIA. Next year in Jerusalem.

DANIEL. Next year in Havana.

SONIA. *(She laughs.)* I thought we needed less stress.

DANIEL. Maybe we should go there.

SONIA. Can we walk there?

DANIEL. Why not?

SONIA. Are you insane?

DANIEL. I'm not trained to think people are insane.

SONIA. I'll never be ready. I left for good. It's over.

DANIEL. Mmm-hmm.

SONIA. It's not a problem for me, you know. It's not. It happened. It's done. I grieved. I'm better. I'm feeling much better. I'll talk to Sam.

DANIEL. You need to.

SONIA. Sam. Oh God, poor Sam. What did I say? You're right. Danny. It's everything, you know. I'm tired. Work, and then this, just, Zak. Why now? He could do anything.

DANIEL. I know.

SONIA. You don't. Stop saying that. You don't know. You don't know.

DANIEL. And you don't know that either. Don't keep pushing me, Sonia. Don't. Because I'm tired too. *(Lights fade.)*

Scene 4

Late night. Jen putting away food, dishes. Very little has been touched. Daniel enters, goes to fridge, drinks milk from carton. Watches Jen clean.

DANIEL. Thank you.

JEN. Couldn't sleep.

DANIEL. I meant the prayer.

JEN. Didn't think I ever paid attention.

DANIEL. You okay?

JEN. You?

DANIEL. Tired.

JEN. Yeah.

DANIEL. I was thinking.

JEN. Uh-oh.

DANIEL. We could still get a week in out at the Keys — go down for some sun. Maybe we could take a long weekend and do some fishing while we're there.

JEN. Who?

DANIEL. You and me.

JEN. At Grampa's?

DANIEL. Why not? Your mom's pretty busy — but I could get away.

JEN. Huh.

DANIEL. What do you think?

JEN. Spinners?

DANIEL. Flies, I think.

JEN. I'm no good at flies.

DANIEL. Practice.

JEN. Mom stays here?

DANIEL. I thought it could just be you and me.

JEN. I can't stand her sometimes.

DANIEL. She can be ... different ...

JEN. Parents split up all the time. Everyone does it. You don't have to lie and pretend that you stay together for the kids —

DANIEL. — No one's talking about that —

JEN. I'm not even going to be here that much longer. Just another year before college.

DANIEL. We're talking about fishing.

JEN. Yeah.

DANIEL. Maybe your brother will come too.

JEN. He's going to war, Dad. Didn't you hear that part?

DANIEL. Everyone doesn't do it.

JEN. What?

DANIEL. Split up.

JEN. Mom's family did.

DANIEL. That's different.

JEN. They sent her away.

DANIEL. No one thought it was a permanent thing. They thought it was for a few months ...

JEN. Why did they?

DANIEL. I don't actually know.

JEN. How does that happen?

DANIEL. I don't know.

JEN. You don't know anything. How did you get to be so old and not know anything?

DANIEL. I don't know.

JEN. The truth is I don't really like fishing —

DANIEL. *(!!!)*

JEN. I just feel bad for the fish, you know. And they never taste as good as the fish from the market. There's all these bones and you can never find them all. I can never get any sleep down there, and everything stays wet the whole time — it's just kind of lame. I don't really want to do it anymore. I'd rather just —

DANIEL. What?

JEN. Go to the water park.

DANIEL. We could go to the water park.

JEN. You and me?

DANIEL. Yeah.

JEN. No way.

DANIEL. I like the water park.

JEN. You're not really invited, though. You go fishing, and I'll go to the water park.

DANIEL. That's not what I had in mind.

JEN. I know.

DANIEL. We're not splitting up. This family doesn't do that. We don't. *(Lights fade.)*

Scene 5

The next morning, Sonia drinks coffee. Zak enters. He's back from running. Gets juice. Drinks from the carton, drains it, exits.

SONIA. Zak? *(He reenters, does not speak. She is trying.)* It's freezing out.

ZAK. Actually, it's a lot colder.

SONIA. Can I make you an omelet or something?

ZAK. Not hungry.

27

SONIA. I was online. Research. Are you interested in, ummm — have you been screened for, officer training or anything like that?

ZAK. I had my physical and all those tests already. They've got me on the list for a few programs. I'm interested in, maybe — mechanical engineering, you know —

SONIA. You did all this already? In Providence?

ZAK. Yeah.

SONIA. It's just that, you didn't say anything. You've been thinking about this a long time?

ZAK. This semester, you know, I've missed you so much, Mom, and I wanted to — it was something I couldn't say on the phone.

SONIA. I was just so …

ZAK. I know.

SONIA. Caught off-guard, you know.

ZAK. Yesterday didn't go like I hoped.

SONIA. No. It wasn't how I thought the day would go either. *(Beat.)* So, what happens next?

ZAK. After I swear in, then I thought I would be home for a few weeks —

SONIA. Great.

ZAK. — Before basic.

SONIA. Basic.

ZAK. Yeah.

SONIA. No, I was just thinking that it's funny. Basic training. Learning some elemental thing, some part of coping. Basic life. I never got that, you know.

ZAK. It's just what they call it.

SONIA. I mean, shouldn't we all get some basic training? *(Sam enters, dressed, with bags and coat. Daniel behind.)*

DANIEL. Sonia —

ZAK. Grampa!

SONIA. Sam, oh, Sam, no.

SAM. I'm heading out.

SONIA. Please stay.

SAM. I think it's best. I just think it's best.

SONIA. I can't begin to tell you how sorry I am —

DANIEL. Please, Dad.

ZAK. Grampa, I was hoping you'd come in with me on Monday.

SAM. I'm in the middle — You and Danny and Zak need to sort this out.

ZAK. I want you to be there. You're the only one who gets it, Papí. You get it. No one else. My friends, my parents.

DANIEL. We'll all go on Monday, Dad.

SAM. I can stay in a hotel.

ZAK. Not alone — I'll come with you —

SONIA. Oh God! My son and my father-in-law spend Christmas in a hotel. My mother would have had a *síncope*.

SAM. Is that like *plotzing? (A moment.)*

SONIA. Sam, please stay.

SAM. I'll stay for coffee.

SONIA. Stay longer. Please. Much longer.

SAM. Coffee and some of that Jell-O salad you always make —

JEN. *(Entering.)* Mom didn't make it this year —

SAM. It's tradition!

JEN. *(Kisses him.)* Morning Papí —

SONIA. We're starting a new tradition this year — all sorts of new traditions. Jen, get your Papí some juice. Let me fix you something to eat. We have lox, bagels, a little whitefish —

SAM. She's Jewish, Danny, she has to be.

DANIEL. That's what I've always said —

JEN. *(She has brought the box of pasteles out, and is untying the string.)* Let's eat these —

ZAK. Suddenly I'm starving.

JEN. Get in line.

SONIA. Oh, they smell so good. We used to have a bakery around the corner — that smell every day walking to school — Mmmm, God. Wow.

SAM. I brought them just to watch her do the "Oh God, wow!"

DANIEL. Funny, chopped liver never had the same effect on me.

SONIA. Guava. This strange hard little fruit. Can't get it anywhere else. Tastes like home.

SAM. Like a good *golabki.*

JEN. What's that, Papí?

SAM. Polish-style cabbage roll.

JEN. Uh-huh?

SAM. Rolled up and stuffed with —

DANIEL. Polenta —

SAM. No, not polenta, it's ground meat and rice —

DANIEL. Polenta —

SAM. Not polenta! Enough with the — ! What is that? No — this

29

is wonderful. We got them on Second Avenue after the war, but nothing like what we got at home —

ZAK. Papí, how old were you again? When you left Poland. How'd you do it?

SAM. Who has a choice? I had to. Fourteen? Fifteen? It's funny how you forget. Fifteen, I think. Fourteen? You know, it was easy for me. Compared to some.

JEN. Easy?

SAM. My uncle and his family were here already. That part was easy.

ZAK. And then you fought —

SAM. Well, that was easy too. I suppose, to some degree, that decision just made itself. You know, a young man, what are my prospects? And this animal in Europe — well. I suppose it was all pretty straightforward.

DANIEL. That's not what you get a Purple Heart for.

SAM. I don't mean the action is straightforward, just the motion. You do what you have to do.

ZAK. Because you want to.

SAM. You have to.

ZAK. I want to. I'm ready. Mom? Can you understand that? I look around, and I know it's where I should be. It's the one true thing that I know — I'm ready. Dad?

DANIEL. What we've always wanted, your mother and I, was for you to make your own — Zacariah, we are so proud of you. (Silence. Sonia rises for more coffee.)

SAM. Give your mother time, Zak, she's a hell of a woman. She'll come around. Not many of us could start over from scratch like she did —

ZAK. You did.

SAM. Not the same thing. When I left Poland, I knew I wasn't ever coming back.

ZAK. But you did go back, Grampa — you went to war.

SAM. That wasn't going home.

ZAK. I don't get it. How could you just let it go like that?

SAM. I never let it go —

ZAK. I would never let that happen.

SONIA. Let's hope you never have to.

ZAK. I don't think "hope" has anything to do with it.

SONIA. Touché.

ZAK. Mom — why don't you ever talk about it?

SONIA. More war stories?

ZAK. What does that mean?

DANIEL. I think your mother means that she made her peace, and you need to respect that.

SONIA. It doesn't have any relevance in my life anymore.

ZAK. Did it ever occur to you that that's just wrong?

SONIA. That I'm wrong about what?

ZAK. Nothing.

SONIA. No, you meant something. What did you mean? What am I wrong about? Besides, oh, everything. What else am I wrong about? The military-industrial complex? The Geneva Convention? NATO?

JEN. Here we go again.

DANIEL. Hey hey, more listening here —

ZAK. You're wrong that it doesn't affect you. You're wrong that it's buried. You're wrong that you walked away from it.

SONIA. What has happened to you?

ZAK. You do nothing.

SAM. Zacariah!

SONIA. Who does nothing?

DANIEL. Stop it, both of you.

ZAK. Well, someone's fucking up my country.

DANIEL. Hey —

ZAK. And I'm not going to run. I'm going to do something. I would have done something —

SONIA. I did not run. I was sent.

ZAK. Whatever —

SONIA. Not the same thing —

ZAK. Like you ever even talk about it — like you ever tell us anything —

JEN. Don't, Mom —

DANIEL. You're way out of bounds, Zak. You have no right — no right at all.

ZAK. I think it's time for someone to look around at what we have, and go, this is worth sacrificing for. Grampa did. He went to war for it. What did you ever give up?

SONIA. I gave up plenty. Don't you call me out about paying dues, because I have paid them.

DANIEL. Apologize to your mother.

ZAK. And you — you said you'd help me with this. You said you'd help me get her to understand, but you just cut and run, as soon as she gets going, you check right out — I am so glad I'm getting out of here —

SONIA. You know what? You'll find this out on your own some godawful day, and I'm sure you won't remember that you heard it here first. But some things are not forgivable. Some things cannot be forgiven. Even when you love the person. Do you hear me? Some things must be forgotten. Forgotten. And I feel — I just think — that this is one of those things. Not the words. The actions. Because the truth is, Zak, if you go. If you go, I do not forgive you. I will never forgive you.

SAM. You can't mean that. You mustn't mean that.

SONIA. I do.

JEN. Mom.

SAM. Listen to me, Sonia, stop now — Danny —

SONIA. The things you've forgotten, Sam. What are they? Can you tell him? The things you put aside, that you cut out of yourself to survive. You never talk about it, Sam, but I know it's there. I recognize it in you. I know.

SAM. There are things you forget.

SONIA. Tell him, Sam.

SAM. Things you have to forget, Zak. Things I've seen. That I've done — My God, but Sonia — these things, if I didn't do them, who would? How could I stand here and look my child in the eye if I had done nothing?

SONIA. It's not nothing — living a good life is not nothing. I'm not asking him not to fight, I'm saying fight here! Read between the lines, damn it, can't you see through the lies — can't you see? This is what they do — they turn children — they turn children against you, against the people who love them most — this is how it starts —

DANIEL. He's not turned, Sonia. Listen to what you're saying — he's not turned —

JEN. Mom — stop it, you're the one who's pushing him out the door —

SONIA. The things I haven't told you, Zak. There are things that I know about what freedom costs.

ZAK. So tell me then. Tell me. (*Sonia isolated in light. Her words come in a torrent —)*

SONIA. I told that priest that I wouldn't go to another home. I wouldn't go to a home with a mother and father. I told them that I had a mother and father, and I didn't need any more. They were placing us all over the country. This is such a big country, you know. I hated all the places, I said no to everything. Wisconsin was at the end of the alphabet. That was all that was left. My mother promised she would come within the year. She wrote. She talked about the weather in her letters. There is not that much to say about the weather in the tropics. Hot today. Rain this afternoon. Hot today. Rain this afternoon. Hot today. She died. Our house-keeper got out. I don't know how she found me. She told me every-thing. She said they both died. They never came. *(Scene resumes.)*

ZAK. Mom, tell me!

SONIA. I can't. *(Beat.)*

ZAK. Jenny, give me a ride downtown. I'm going to Joey's. I can stay there until Monday, when I swear in.

JEN. I'll get my bag.

SAM. Don't leave like this, Zak. Daniel, say something to him. Danny.

DANIEL. Do you need any money?

ZAK. I'll be fine.

DANIEL. Here, take some.

SAM. Sonia. Bless your son before he goes. Give him your blessing. Nothing he has said or done, nothing could possibly — I beg you.

JEN. Come on, brother.

ZAK. They have a program, you know, the Marines, when you sign up. Accelerated. You can go right in. There's no place for me here anymore. I really thought, I really really thought. I don't know. I had this insane idea that what I wanted mattered to you. That what I saw in my future was. Important. I thought. Grampa? *(He exits, followed by Jen and Samuel. Sonia stands, immobile. Daniel watches his family exit, turns back to his wife.)*

DANIEL. I love you. But I can't reach you anymore. I don't know you anymore. Your face is different. Your hands, even your smell. I see you there, but I can't find you. All this anger. Why? I'm going now. Sonia. I'm going with Zak.

SONIA. And then what?

DANIEL. I don't know.

SONIA. What does that mean, you don't know?

DANIEL. I don't know. *(Daniel exits. Lights fade into a spot on Sonia.)*

SONIA. My mother used to read me a book. In Spanish it was called *Pedro Pan*. The boy who could fly. Neverland. The lost children. Wendy was the mother to them all. And she told them stories about the lives they had left behind. So they wouldn't forget. And one day, Peter got sad, and he missed home so much that he flew back there, across the ocean. He flew to the window of his bedroom. But his mother had locked it. And he couldn't get back in. I always used to wonder, what kind of a terrible mother would do that? Even after years and years, wouldn't you keep the window open? Even through blizzard and rain and heat and locusts, wouldn't you keep the window open? In case? Just in case? Wouldn't you? Would I? *(Lights fade.)*

Scene 6

The desert. A military convoy. The lights are tightly focused on the pair inside the vehicle. Zak and Nina in the truck. Nina drives.

NINA. Not me. In six months, I'm posted to Fort Living Room — and then I'll be back at the tracks.

ZAK. You feeling lucky, Nina?

NINA. Hell no — it's for the dogs. My sister emailed — there's six more greys up for adoption. We're gonna turn the back lot into a kennel and just keep them. As many as we can. It's savage, you know. They keep them in these tiny cages, and they jack them up on speed. Sport, my ass.

ZAK. I didn't know.

NINA. You with me?

ZAK. Yeah.

NINA. I need you to drive soon. I'm wasted.

ZAK. This doesn't look right.

NINA. MSR Eagle.

ZAK. Yeah. MSR Eagle. But, it doesn't look right.

NINA. It all looks the same to me.

ZAK. Fuck.

NINA. What?

ZAK. I just remembered.

NINA. What?

ZAK. My little sister's birthday.

NINA. Fuck you! Don't fucking do that!

ZAK. Sorry.

NINA. You scared the piss out of me.

ZAK. Sorry.

NINA. Save "fuck" for when you need it. *(Lights up on Sonia. She sleeps alone on the couch. Sonia writhes in her sleep.)* Can't see shit.

ZAK. I never had a dog. Always wanted one.

NINA. Those Frogs? I've never seen gouging like that, the sand just chewed through the rotors — I mean you can't fix that — you can grind it down, but you can't ever get it like new again. And Jimmy Chee, you know he's been waiting on that flak jacket since deportation, you know the guy —

ZAK. Couldn't close it or some shit?

NINA. James is super-sized — XXL — and they get the new shipment in, Jimmy's going on about, "Now I got my jacket, bring 'em on!" And it turns out that instead of flak jackets, they sent canteens — You believe that?

ZAK. I'd rather have a canteen than a jacket any day.

NINA. What're you gonna fill it with, asshole?

ZAK. Shit.

NINA. Cut it out, man.

ZAK. You hear that?

NINA. No.

ZAK. I heard something.

NINA. I can't hear shit over this piece of shit motor

ZAK. That's what I mean. Sounded like a belt broke or something.

NINA. Running okay. *(The engine coughs, sputters, dies.)*

ZAK. Wait.

NINA. I'll fix it

ZAK. I want to check coordinates. Something's wrong.

NINA. We're not in a hot area, girlfriend. It's been cleared already.

ZAK. Hear that?

NINA. You are so spooked today. What is it? *(The sound of gunfire.)*

ZAK.
Ohio, this is Shakespeare.
We are taking fire at Bravo
Roma 4260/1245

NINA.
Helmet. Jacket. Shit. *(She is try-ing to start the truck, which will not turn over.)* Come on, baby. Come on.

ZAK. Do you copy? *(The sound of gunfire.)* Bravo Roma 4260 —
NINA. Turn over, bitch — Turn over!
ZAK. 1245 — *(The sound of gunfire. Sonia sits up, crying out.)*
SONIA. Zak!
NINA. They're in front of us.
ZAK. They're coming up behind.
NINA. How the fuck — this area's been cleared!
ZAK. We are taking fire at 4260/1245 *(Sound of explosions.)*
NINA. How the fuck —
SONIA. I'm here, baby. I'm here.
ZAK. Can you engage? Repeat.
NINA. Oh shit. Here we go. Oh shit is my shepherd. I shall not want —
ZAK. Can you engage?
NINA. — He leadeth me beside the fuck oh fuck —
ZAK. Nina!
NINA. There, look there —
ZAK. Soldier!
NINA. The sand —
ZAK. Look at that!
NINA. It's so beautiful. *(They stare at something huge and beautiful. An enormous explosion. The sky burns. Blackout on Nina and Zak.)*
SONIA. Forgive me. I'll tell you, I'll tell you everything.

End of Act One

36

ACT TWO

Prologue

Zak appears as at end of Act One, in military fatigues, and stands in a pool of light.

ZAK. It was the loudest thing I ever heard. And bright. I was surprised. Your whole life people tell you about how things are supposed to be, and they almost never are. But this was. RPGs are bright. And I thought, fuck, I wish I was home, watching cable. Or bugging my sister. Or. Just home. My mom. I thought, This is going to kill my mom. You know, when the recruiter talked to me, he kept saying how the girls were everywhere. Women. You know. And they'd do whatever you wanted. How you could get a girl everywhere you went. Korea, the Balkans, even, you know, out here. And that's not why I signed up. Not at all. Still, I was, I have to say, looking forward to it. Stupid. I never even made it to my first leave.

Scene 1

Havana, 1961. Marta cleans. Pilar enters with boxes of pastries.

PILAR. Hurry hurry, get the door behind me.
MARTA. What's this?
PILAR. Hurry, before the whole neighborhood sees!
MARTA. What have you done?
PILAR. *Pasteles! Pasteles de guayava* —
MARTA. Did you rob a bank?
PILAR. For Sonia's birthday.

37

MARTA. How did you ever —

PILAR. I have ways, Marta, I have my ways. We may have socialized our factories, but *pasteles* belong to those with connections!

MARTA. Shameless!

PILAR. Come, Marta, come and taste them.

MARTA. I couldn't —

PILAR. One. A taste.

MARTA. *Ay!*

PILAR. Sit. They're still warm. Oh I can hardly believe it. We can each have one, and there will be plenty left for a birthday lunch. Two weeks, Marta, two weeks of smiling at that fat baker, "Do you have *pasteles?*" and every day, "No, *señora*, not today." The man bakes morning, noon, and night, where do they all go? But yesterday — I wore my houndstooth suit — you know the one —

MARTA. Yes!

PILAR. Two sizes too small — "Any *pasteles* today?" He looked me over, and said, "Come back tomorrow, bring me a kiss. A little kiss is all I ask."

MARTA. Shameless!

PILAR. Two dozen *pasteles* for one kiss seems fair. This morning, I didn't brush my teeth. Disgusting.

MARTA. For Sonia, it's worth it.

PILAR. Eat slowly, Marta. Make it last.

MARTA. Mmmm.

PILAR. God … wow …

MARTA. A small piece of eternity.

PILAR. Fifteen, Marta! Fifteen. Can you believe it?

MARTA. I can't.

PILAR. Do you remember my sweet fifteen?

MARTA. Everything.

PILAR. My father filled the house with songbirds.

MARTA. What a mess they made!

PILAR. And we had twenty-five couples for a dinner dance, everyone in white. My first taste of champagne. We already had nothing, but he still made the day magical.

MARTA. Your poor father.

PILAR. Not a businessman.

MARTA. Not a businessman.

PILAR. He didn't need a new government to take his business. He lost it all by himself.

MARTA. May he rest in peace.

PILAR. Amen.

MARTA. White roses.

PILAR. Yes, you put them in my hair.

MARTA. I can do that for her. We don't have roses for her, but any flower will do.

PILAR. And the *pasteles.*

MARTA. And the *pasteles.*

PILAR. I'll give her my ring. I have to give her something. *(They finish eating in silence.)*

MARTA. I can't get that stain out of the sink.

PILAR. Leave it.

MARTA. I changed all the linens — that's how your father liked it — twice a week —

PILAR. And the lessons?

MARTA. *Ay, Señora,* I tried.

PILAR. A little bit every day, Marta.

MARTA. We still have a cake to bake.

PILAR. *(She pulls the newspaper out, and lays it across the table.)* Let's begin here. With the big letters. Look here, this is simple enough. And a big picture —

MARTA. What pretty girls.

PILAR. Go ahead. You know that one.

MARTA. Woo. Woom —

PILAR. Womb is a part of her. The beginning of the word, and of life. Go on.

MARTA. Women.

PILAR. Women! "W" — women and world and womb. What do you think of that?

MARTA. I know this "M" — the other side of "W" — M — like mother —

PILAR. Or man — the other side of "woman" —

MARTA. But this word is too long.

PILAR. Break it down.

MARTA. Help me —

PILAR. *Compañera* — I help by not helping.

MARTA. Sounds very *yanqui* to me.

PILAR. Go on —

MARTA. Mob. Ill. Zz? What is that "zz" doing there?

PILAR. Mobilized. Women mobilized.

MARTA. What?

PILAR. Women mobilized.

MARTA. Means what?

PILAR. I don't know. Women mobilized. Women moving. Let me see ... "Women mobilized ... The first battalion of women teachers has been mobilized to Aguas Frías for the launch of the Education Initiative. Women and girls as young as thirteen are traveling to the provinces to assist in the education of all Cubans."

MARTA. Look at them. Wearing pants.

PILAR. Work in the country is hard.

MARTA. Prostitutes — that's what they'll become —

PILAR. They're teaching people to read, old woman! If they had done this with you, I wouldn't have my hands full!

MARTA. Out there, unsupervised — why is it only the girls, eh?

PILAR. Don't be ridiculous. Young men go too.

MARTA. Idiot mothers. Idiots. I know what happens when a girl, alone, with a boy — at thirteen? At sixteen?

PILAR. When then?

MARTA. Never! Sixty! Old!

PILAR. Things are changing —

MARTA. Things have been changing since before I was born, and everything is still the same as it ever was. A girl belongs at home.

PILAR. Now wait, these people, no schools, no teachers, do you think that's fair?

MARTA. What about Sonia?

PILAR. What about Sonia?

MARTA. Would you send her where the devil cried out three times and no one heard him?

PILAR. Sonia?

MARTA. In the back of a jeep, to Asshole Province — in pants? Would you send her?

PILAR. What's gotten into you?

MARTA. I'll take out my eyes the day I see Sonia on the back of a military truck. *(Silence.)*

PILAR. *(Pilar begins putting the pasteles away.)* I thought we could go to the beach later on, Marta, do you think we could get a picnic together?

MARTA. I am sorry. These things.

PILAR. Yes.

MARTA. I feel them deeply.

40

PILAR. I know.

MARTA. I must seem ungrateful to you.

PILAR. Not at all.

MARTA. I am so very grateful. All the trouble I cause.

PILAR. What trouble? You don't eat anything, like a little bird, you only nibble. No trouble, Marta.

MARTA. I keep the copper coins in the corner — to bring you good fortune. Flowers, rum for Oshún —

PILAR. *(Affectionately.)* Ay, Marta. What will we do with you? In a hundred years, you will be exactly the same.

MARTA. I don't like change. You won't send Sonia?

PILAR. No, Marta. *(Beat.)* Any news from your husband?

MARTA. No.

PILAR. I'm sorry.

MARTA. A mechanic — what could he know? They tore the shop apart. If they think they'll find money, ha-ha — no — he never made any money in his life. No charges — what do they think he knows? How to fix what's broken. He's never said a word against anyone.

PILAR. Mistakes get made all the time —

MARTA. I know.

PILAR. I want to help. In whatever way I can. Orfeo, too. Stay with us. As long as you need to.

MARTA. Thank you

PILAR. I want to help. But the walls.

MARTA. Yes.

PILAR. It's a difficult time for all of us, you know, Marta. We just have to be a little more careful.

MARTA. Yes. I understand.

PILAR. You can say anything to me. But remember the walls. The walls in this house are thin. *(Lights fade. Possible sounds of radio broadcast — an intermingling of U.S. and Cuban — music, speeches.)*

Scene 2

Young Sonia and Pilar. They are dressing Young Sonia in her in her Association of Rebel Youth uniform (military style with red neck scarf). Orfeo listens to a radio.

YOUNG SONIA. Why so ugly?

PILAR. Hush.

YOUNG SONIA. I look like a boy.

PILAR. Better that way.

YOUNG SONIA. Let me wear my new shoes, Mamá.

PILAR. Boots, Sonia. Everyone will have on their boots.

ORFEO. He's speaking — Kennedy is speaking — shhh.

YOUNG SONIA. I hate that Radio Swan — music, Papá. The Twist!

PILAR. What is he saying?

ORFEO. Stop talking so I can hear —

YOUNG SONIA. Mamá? More here.

PILAR. Leave it!

YOUNG SONIA. You're doing it wrong! Why can't Marta do it?

MARTA. *(Calling from offstage —)* I'd rather die.

YOUNG SONIA. You're doing it wrong — oww!

PILAR. That's what happens when you —

YOUNG SONIA. You did that on purpose!

PILAR. Let me see — there, no blood.

YOUNG SONIA. There is blood — look, get a bandage —

PILAR. You are so exaggerated —

YOUNG SONIA. You want me to look terrible!

ORFEO. It's hard to make out —

MARTA. *(Entering.)* I like that Kennedy — so handsome — what does he say?

YOUNG SONIA. Well, he's not as handsome as Fidel.

ORFEO. Something about democracy —

YOUNG SONIA. Mamá? Don't you think Fidel is handsome?

PILAR. He can't dance. What do you do with a man who can't dance?

YOUNG SONIA. Well, I think he is very handsome.

ORFEO. That's too tight.

YOUNG SONIA. Papá —

ORFEO. Too tight.

YOUNG SONIA. But —

PILAR. Like your father says.

YOUNG SONIA. Stop treating me like a baby.

PILAR. Stop acting like one.

YOUNG SONIA. It's not fair.

PILAR. Stupid rallies

YOUNG SONIA. Papá!

PILAR. The beach would be so much more fun than a rally. Marta made us a picnic —

YOUNG SONIA. But all my friends will be there.

MARTA. Friends! What friends! All her friends are gone to Miami.

YOUNG SONIA. I have new friends!

ORFEO. Nothing more. Big talk. Liberation is coming. Blah blah blah.

PILAR. Music, Orfeo. Put on *Radio Mambí.*

ORFEO. Let me sing you a little song, my dove. A song about love … a song about liberty —

YOUNG SONIA. Elvis, Papá. Let me try. *(She scans the stations. Radio static, a mix of speeches, songs, then "Veinte Años" or another popular tune from the 1930s–40s.*)*

MARTA. That's a good one — that one there —

YOUNG SONIA. If you're a hundred years old — let me find a better one —

ORFEO. Come. My darling … *(During the following, Orfeo takes Pilar and they dance, while Marta and Young Sonia watch. Music, dancing, talking, singing — all overlapping — Orfeo sings along to the radio. They dance.)*

PILAR. Now this man, he can dance. *(Orfeo dips her.)* Shameless!

YOUNG SONIA. Mamá — teach me, like that — like that — *(She cuts in and dances with Pilar.)*

PILAR. The man holds you here —

ORFEO. Not so tight —

YOUNG SONIA. That's how you do it —

PILAR. That's how you do it —

ORFEO. *(Turning off the radio.)* Sonia — it's time — the rally's already started.

---

* See Special Note on Songs and Recordings on copyright page.

YOUNG SONIA. Papí — let me stay —

PILAR. Let's go to the beach instead —

ORFEO. Rally first. Beach later.

PILAR. But Papí —

ORFEO. This is important.

PILAR. But she doesn't really have to go — on her birthday?

ORFEO. She has to go.

PILAR. Sonia, get your bathing suit and let's go to Varadero —

ORFEO. Listen to me — listen, both of you. Pilar — *(Grabbing her arm.)*

PILAR. You're hurting me —

ORFEO. Sonia has go to this rally. Today more than ever.

PILAR. Why today?

YOUNG SONIA. I'll go, Mamá, I want to go, it's all right —

ORFEO. Pilar — please, listen — *(A knock on the door.)*

PILAR. *(Calling.)* Marta — would you?

ORFEO. I invited Tito —

PILAR. Why, in God's name?

MARTA. Hide the food.

ORFEO. Sonia, go finish getting dressed. *(Young Sonia exits.)*

PILAR. What is going on?

ORFEO. I had a visit yesterday, at the University.

PILAR. What does that mean? *(Marta enters with Tito.)*

TITO. *Compañera!*

MARTA. You know the way, sir.

PILAR. Tito — you're looking so well! Come have a seat!

TITO. What a day! *(Calling out.)* Where is the birthday girl? — Orfeo — pride suits you, my friend.

PILAR. Marta, some tea —

TITO. I heard a rumor …

PILAR. What rumor?

TITO. Were there birthday *pasteles?*

MARTA. You devil, nothing gets past you!

TITO. The smell. Heavenly.

ORFEO. We have some leftovers. Marta, if you please?

TITO. But surely Marta can stay with us and enjoy our company? Sit, Marta.

MARTA. I am happy to help — I'm staying with the family during my difficulties. You know, my husband.

TITO. Yes. I heard. Surely there has just been some sort of misunderstanding. Perhaps I could put in a word or two.

MARTA. A poor man, all his life, a small shop, nothing of value. A poor dumb man, what could he know?

TITO. Fortunately I know the words that open every door. "Push" and "Pull!"

ORFEO. Marta is like family, Tito. If you could do anything to help.

PILAR. Marta is family!

ORFEO. Come sit, sit with us — have you seen Sonia yet?

TITO. I have not seen her.

YOUNG SONIA. *(Entering completely dressed in her uniform.)* Do I look all right?

MARTA. Like a boy.

YOUNG SONIA. Mamá!

PILAR. Marta?

TITO. Let me be the first to toast — if I may take the liberty —

ORFEO. A toast then.

PILAR. Marta. The glasses please?

TITO. Dear lady, I long for the day when none of us has to work so hard. When Marta won't have to clean and fetch.

MARTA. There will always be dirt to wash —

TITO. But one day, perhaps, Pilar will clean your home —

MARTA. And the President will kiss my —

PILAR. I'll get the glasses. How right you are, Tito — please sit, Marta, you've been on your feet all day.

MARTA. Nonsense.

PILAR. Whiskey? *(A mistake.)*

ORFEO. Rum.

TITO. Come, Martita, by me.

MARTA. I don't drink.

TITO. But surely, today of all days?

YOUNG SONIA. If we could take in a little bit more right here, don't you think that would help, Papá?

TITO. To be fifteen, and in bloom. What I wouldn't give to have the world — right there — right at my fingertips — The things you will see, Sonia, in your lifetime —

ORFEO. Get the glasses, Pilar —

PILAR. And how are you enjoying the Delgados' home?

TITO. Dear lady, it now belongs to the People.

MARTA. Then why are you the only "people" living in it?

PILAR. Such a glorious view. Water and sky.

TITO. The suits in the closet — do you know that man had fifty ties? Can you imagine? Fifty? In this heat? Ties? And a cabinet full of ashtrays. One whole cabinet, full of ashtrays. What is the revolution going to do with fifty neckties?

MARTA. I have a good idea — *(She mimes hanging herself.)*

PILAR. *(Returning with the drinks on a tray.)* Marta! Your drink. And for you, and you …

YOUNG SONIA. And me?

TITO. On such a day as this …

PILAR. Orfeo?

ORFEO. On such a day as this …

YOUNG SONIA. Can I really?

PILAR. *(Handing Young Sonia her drink.)* Careful now, sip it. *(She gets herself another glass of rum.)*

ORFEO. A toast to Sonia — Come my darling. A birthday toast to you. Tito, will you do the honors?

TITO. I have a better idea. Sonia, You should do it. So much to celebrate? You, a Young Pioneer, and our country free —

YOUNG SONIA. That sounds like a toast already.

TITO. Forgive me. Please, lead us.

ORFEO. Sonia?

YOUNG SONIA. Papí?

ORFEO. What were we just discussing?

YOUNG SONIA. Well, we were speaking about — To have a chance — to change. To know that this is my country, and that we are no longer — Mamá? Is this silly?

PILAR. Go on, my darling.

YOUNG SONIA. To know that it really belongs to us. Once and for all. To Cubans. For people to — I don't know —

TITO. Go on.

YOUNG SONIA. It wasn't right how it was before, don't you agree? But now — It feels so free, now. It feels so right. Into the future! My head is spinning! *(They all echo the final toast "Into the Future!" — Tito overlaps next line.)*

TITO. My lovely lady. My lovely, lovely lady. *(They drink except Marta.)* Sonia. I know the fifteenth-birthday celebration isn't what it once was. No doubt your mother has told you about the lavish affairs in her day. But what we have now, what we are building together is so much more precious. I have little to give, but it comes with much love. *(He presents her with a small box, awkwardly wrapped.)*

PILAR. You shouldn't have. You mustn't, Tito. You spoil her!

YOUNG SONIA. Thank you. *(Opening the present.)*

TITO. It's a little nothing. Something that was given to me in thanks for my service.

YOUNG SONIA. A pin?

TITO. A star. Like those in your smile.

ORFEO. It's too much.

TITO. Forgive me, my friend. I am forward, I know. Even though I am old, I know this special birthday should be remembered in a special way. Forgive me.

YOUNG SONIA. Thank you. I'll wear it to the rally. Thank you.

PILAR. I have something for you as well, my darling. I had hoped to give it to you this afternoon by the sea, which is where my father gave it to me when I turned fifteen.

ORFEO. Pilar —

PILAR. I want to.

ORFEO. My darling —

MARTA. *Señora* ...

PILAR. I will.

YOUNG SONIA. Well, what is it?

TITO. I love surprises.

PILAR. On my fifteenth birthday, my father took me to the beach, and he put this on my finger, as I do yours. And he told me, "My daughter, more precious than gold, wear this. It was worn by your mother and grandmother and her mother before that. Spanish gold. More pure than what you can get now. When you wear it, remember the purity of my love for you, and the strength of the line that binds you to me." Happy birthday, my darling.

YOUNG SONIA. Your finger looks naked without it.

PILAR. Does it fit?

ORFEO. Happy birthday, my dove.

TITO. A beautiful piece. It graces your hand

YOUNG SONIA. Papí. Can I really wear it?

ORFEO. Pilar?

PILAR. It belongs to you. You can do with it what you like.

YOUNG SONIA. Maybe I should save it? I don't know if, at the rally, all those people ...

TITO. Perhaps to leave it for a more ... private time would be wise.

YOUNG SONIA. I'll put it away.

ORFEO. I hate to be the taskmaster, but … Time.

PILAR. Thank you for your visit, Tito, please excuse us —

ORFEO. Sonia, please run and get your banner.

MARTA. You have to get your things together. *(Sonia and Pilar exit.)*

TITO. Thank you for gracing us. *(Marta exits.)* I too must run. One more — between us — *(He pours another drink.)* The place is looking lovely, but bare. I have some posters. Perhaps you would like some?

ORFEO. Posters. Yes.

TITO. Such a fine bottle, where do you manage to find such good rum?

ORFEO. Bring some banners too, my friend.

TITO. Treasure that child. Orfeo, pride suits you. I'll make sure my next report — well, you know, I'll make sure I mention it all. By the way, there are opportunities — for volunteers, you understand — men and women — especially those with doubts, you see — to re-commit themselves. But seeing as you and your family are so patri-otic — I don't suppose you would be interested? Perhaps Marta? Two months in the country. Sugar cane. Think about it. I must run …

ORFEO. Don't forget the posters.

TITO. Of course, my friend. Goodbye.

ORFEO. Goodbye. *(Tito exits.)* Goodbye. Goodbye. Pilar?

PILAR. *(Returning.)* I'm here

ORFEO. Why must you bait him?

PILAR. She is my daughter too.

ORFEO. One word from him —

PILAR. Him? A farmer's son. A spy! A nobody. Living in that house, that house he stole —

ORFEO. They fled. If they had stayed, they would still have their fifty ties.

PILAR. They were our friends, Orfeo. We watched them leave, with one suitcase each. Carrying their hearts in their hands. And him in there, in that house, counting the silverware, counting the ashtrays. I'll go blind before he'll touch one hair on my daughter's head.

ORFEO. Control yourself.

PILAR. How dare he come in here and shame us in front of Sonia — a red star — I'll drop before I see her wear a red star — And you — sycophant! Hanger-on. *(He strikes her.)*

ORFEO. Not a word.

PILAR. What have I done?

ORFEO. My darling … *(He kisses her.)* Sit down and rest. The heat is too much. You must rest quiet. Quiet, Pilar.

PILAR. You get smaller every day. All of you. All of us, we hold our breath, watch the skies, wait for a sign. How long will we wait?

ORFEO. For your own good. For our good. My dove. It is only a pin. We have to be smart. For just a little while longer. *(Marta and Young Sonia entering. Young Sonia enters, pulling leaves out of her pockets.)*

MARTA. Take it out now!

YOUNG SONIA. Mamá! Don't you think it looks better now?

MARTA. Socks in her bra!

YOUNG SONIA. She's filling my pockets with basil —

MARTA. Tito's put that evil eye all over you —

ORFEO. Marta, please!

PILAR. *(Sharply.)* Stop it, the two of you. Like children all day long!

MARTA. My apologies. But her bra! You know?

ORFEO. Sonia, honestly. *(Young Sonia removes, then hands over the socks.)*

YOUNG SONIA. Mamá? Mamá what is it?

PILAR. I am tired.

ORFEO. Rest, my dove.

YOUNG SONIA. Is she crying? Why is she crying?

ORFEO. I'll go with you today. Let me hold the banner —

YOUNG SONIA. But it's for the young people —

ORFEO. I am young! A young man, with my life ahead of me. And you need an escort.

MARTA. Just take a few leaves. In your pocket.

ORFEO. Let's go.

YOUNG SONIA. All my friends will be there.

ORFEO. I'll keep my distance. Just pretend I am an old lap dog that needs a pat every once in a while.

PILAR. Sonia — do what they ask. Smile at the soldiers. Wave the banners. Be home soon.

MARTA. For your cake.

YOUNG SONIA. Orange?

MARTA. With flowers.

YOUNG SONIA. Bye-bye, Mamá. Marta.

MARTA. A kiss. *(Young Sonia kisses Marta's cheek.)*

YOUNG SONIA. Are you sure you're…?

PILAR. Right as rain. Be careful. *(Young Sonia and Orfeo exit.)* I am so tired. I'll go lie down.

MARTA. Let me get you some ice.

PILAR. Whatever for?

MARTA. You have a heat rash. Here. I know just what you need. *(She goes to the ice box and wraps some ice in a towel. Gently places ice on Pilar's face.)* This unbearable inferno. Only April and another six months to go. Ice. A yellow towel. For Oshún.

PILAR. That feels better.

MARTA. Your mother never cared for the heat. When she was pregnant, it was the fan, and her feet and hands in a bucket of ice. And me all day long bringing more ice into the house. She told me that in America, everything is covered with ice all year long.

PILAR. Ice?

MARTA. And that it falls from the sky. Like candy.

PILAR. I dream of snow. Clean and cold. Tiny crystals that make a sound like music.

MARTA. Just like your Mamá.

PILAR. Am I a good wife?

MARTA. And a good mother. If your mother had lived to see you … But she didn't.

PILAR. I think I cannot continue, Marta.

MARTA. Wake up, Pilar. Look and see. Sonia. Rallies. Your husband —

PILAR. My husband —

MARTA. Sonia in a uniform?

PILAR. Something happened. He couldn't tell me.

MARTA. I made a pledge to your mother, on the night you were born. Let me speak —

PILAR. This stupid world, stupid rallies, you'll see, it won't last.

MARTA. There was so much blood that night. You, born perfect, with a full head of hair — you didn't cry at all. But your mother, still bleeding. She drenched the sheets.

PILAR. Please stop.

MARTA. And I held her closed. I held tight to her flesh inside, trying to stop the blood — your father ran to get the doctor back — and we waited, the three of us. You sleeping, and your mother, so pale. She asked for water and I couldn't get it for her, do you hear that? I couldn't let go, for fear of the …

PILAR. Yes.

MARTA. I couldn't help her.

PILAR. I was born into your hands.

MARTA. Yes.

PILAR. And Sonia was born in your hands.

MARTA. If he ever strikes you when I am in the room —

PILAR. He doesn't strike me.

MARTA. — So help me, by *Santa Barbara*. I'll fix him so nothing ever works right again.

PILAR. I love him.

MARTA. I swore that night, on your mother's blood.

PILAR. We have to get through these times, Marta, together. *(Beat.)*

MARTA. Changes! Everything — it was terrible before, but we knew what the rules were. Now — we whisper for Tito? For a fool like him? Sonia, in pants — and your husband, I cannot say his name — banners? Can't you see?

PILAR. I can't.

MARTA. These stupid men. When I was a girl, the men were as big as trees. When they walked, the earth moved. Now, they scurry like rats. Who left these men in charge of anything?

PILAR. You mustn't talk that way. I know you love your husband.

MARTA. My poor husband. Happy are those with low expectations —

PILAR. They'll never be disappointed ...

MARTA. I am a foolish old woman. A life spent in foolishness.

PILAR. The pair of us.

MARTA. They came at night — the rats — scratching at the door, and they took him away. A man as big as a cannon, and they took him.

PILAR. No charges?

MARTA. Señora.

PILAR. What haven't you told me? Why is he in jail? You know, Marta.

MARTA. I don't know anything.

PILAR. Why are you lying to me, old woman? Tell me. *(A beat.)*

MARTA. He was working. Repairs. At the airport. Not planes, you know, he's too stupid for that, but the wagons, the cars, other things. He saw, one day he came home and he told me, he had seen ...

PILAR. What? What did he see?

MARTA. Children. It was every day. Ten children, or twenty children. Walking to the planes. Alone, you know, not the families. Little ones. Crying. And his heart, you know, everything makes that man cry, everything.

PILAR. Getting on the planes?

MARTA. They're getting out. He asked — quietly, he asked. He's not a fool, you know, he's sly — there are seats on every flight for them — to Miami.

PILAR. But how? With the embassy closed it's nearly impossible to get visas. It's impossible to travel —

MARTA. They make — people are making —

PILAR. What people? What are they making?

MARTA. They were meeting late at night — I didn't know — I didn't know what he was doing — they would come to the shop late and sit up all night making false ones — It's a special visa — for children. With the stamp and everything —

PILAR. He falsified passports? In your house?

MARTA. They can't prove it —

PILAR. They took him away!

MARTA. He gave me a box to hide.

PILAR. And you have brought this thing into my house? You said your heart was broken — that you were lonely —

MARTA. I didn't think I could tell you.

PILAR. Do you want us all in prison? Do you know what they do to women in prison?

MARTA. There's no proof —

PILAR. But they took him away!

MARTA. They can't keep him — they can't hold him, they have no proof —

PILAR. They need no proof! They're watching you! They're watching us all.

MARTA. I pray to *Santa Barbara,* we are all under her protection — nothing can happen to us —

PILAR. This is how you repay my mother — how you keep your pledge — like this? Where is this box — these visas — no don't tell me — are they safe? Are they safe? *(Marta nods.)* Make me one.

MARTA. Don't send Sonia.

PILAR. Orfeo wants her to go to the provinces. I know it.

MARTA. If Sonia leaves, they'll know about my husband, they'll have the proof they need —

PILAR. You talk, Marta. You talk. But you do nothing. The Devil take your soul.

MARTA. I cannot.

PILAR. On the blood of my mother, you can.

MARTA. Pilar! I cannot write. I can't read.

PILAR. Did you see your husband working. Did you watch him?

MARTA. Yes.

PILAR. Show me what he did. For Sonia. For Sonia you can.

(Lights fade.)

Scene 3

Young Sonia and José. They rally. They hide behind a pillar in a corner and whisper. The sound of speeches behind them. Periodically shouts are heard. They turn and wave banners, but go back to the conversation. Young Sonia and José wave their banners.

JOSÉ. I have a present for you.

YOUNG SONIA. What is it?

JOSÉ. It's one of a kind, but I have hundreds to give. You can't wear it, but it will keep you warm, and you cannot buy it, although it's more precious than money.

YOUNG SONIA. I don't like your riddles. *(Shouts from the crowd.)*

JOSÉ. I can't come out and say.

YOUNG SONIA. Just put the box in my hand.

JOSÉ. It doesn't come in a box.

YOUNG SONIA. It's a cat?

JOSÉ. No.

YOUNG SONIA. Is it alive? A plant — a shell?

JOSÉ. It's alive. I think it could be.

YOUNG SONIA. I'm tired of this game. Tell me or I'm going home.

JOSÉ. Close your eyes.

YOUNG SONIA. Where is my father?

JOSÉ. He can't see us. Close your eyes.

YOUNG SONIA. It better not be a toad or a beetle. *(She closes her eyes.)*

JOSÉ. Now hold very still. *(He kisses her.)*
YOUNG SONIA. I didn't get it. You should give it to me again. *(He kisses her again.)* Better than sugar cane.
JOSÉ. You liked it?
YOUNG SONIA. Yes. *(He kisses her again. Shouts from the crowd.)* My father! I have to go! *(She waves her banner.)*
JOSÉ. He's listening to the speeches.
YOUNG SONIA. And we should be too.
JOSÉ. Is that why you came today?
YOUNG SONIA. I wanted to listen to the speeches … and see you. *(Shouts from the crowd.)*
JOSÉ. I'm going to marry you. On your sixteenth birthday, I'm going to marry you Sonia.
YOUNG SONIA. Shameless — what makes you think I want to? What makes you think I'm not a new woman, who wants to wear pants and live in the jungle. What if I cut my hair and grow a beard? What then?
JOSÉ. You are free, *mariposa,* to be who you choose to be.
YOUNG SONIA. What if I dance the Twist?
JOSÉ. This is a revolution with *pachanga.* Anything goes!
YOUNG SONIA. *(Singing.)*
   Come on baby, Let's do the twist
   Come on baby, Let's do the twist
   Come on now, it goes like this.
JOSÉ. Show me more.
YOUNG SONIA. *Come on baby —*
JOSÉ. Do it again.
YOUNG SONIA. *Let's do the twist.*
JOSÉ. Not so fast. Slower, so I can watch you.
YOUNG SONIA. You do it.
JOSÉ. *Come on baby, let's do the twist —*
YOUNG SONIA. Hold me here …
JOSÉ. A free woman.
YOUNG SONIA. A free man.
JOSÉ. Come with me to the Sierra. I leave next week. Have you spoken to Tito? Three months in the provinces. We work all day, and at night, sit together at the same table, drink from the same cup. Three months to linger in your embrace, drown in your eyes.
YOUNG SONIA. My parents will never let me go.
JOSÉ. You don't need their permission.

YOUNG SONIA. You know Tito — ask him. Ask him to talk to my father. Ask him — he can explain it to them better than I can.
JOSÉ. Where did you learn to dance like that? Where did you learn that song?
YOUNG SONIA. My father has a radio.
JOSÉ. But I've never heard that song —
YOUNG SONIA. It's a special radio. He gets the broadcasts from Radio Swan. I get the music.
JOSÉ. But this isn't allowed. Radio Swan isn't allowed.
YOUNG SONIA. It's just a radio.
JOSÉ. Your father has a radio.
YOUNG SONIA. He doesn't use it for anything like that. Don't look at me like that. It's just a radio. *(Shouts from the crowd. There is the sound of gunfire.)* What was that?
VOICES. *Paredón! (A roar from the crowd.)*
JOSÉ. Look at that! *(Gunfire.)*
YOUNG SONIA. Oh my God. I know that man!
JOSÉ. Look at that! *(Gunfire. Lights fade.)*

Scene 4

Pilar and Orfeo. At home.

PILAR. How many?
ORFEO. Four men.
PILAR. Did she see?
ORFEO. I don't know.
PILAR. You took her to that place —
ORFEO. I thought they would sing songs. *(Silence.)* She won't ever go back.
PILAR. We agree, then. *(Silence.)*
ORFEO. There are rumors.
PILAR. Yes?
ORFEO. Soon, my dove. Very soon.
PILAR. Yes.
ORFEO. No more rallies for Sonia. I can go. Show my face there.

Show support. It's important now. That things have changed.

PILAR. She has changed.

ORFEO. Sonia?

PILAR. She watches us now. Watches everything. Like she's taking notes. Dear God, am I saying this? I think she talks to Tito. I think she tells him things.

ORFEO. No.

PILAR. Forgive me. The things a mother knows — She talks constantly of leaving us. Marrying, or going to the provinces, of the future constantly. I am losing her.

ORFEO. As it must be.

PILAR. No! Not this way! Not her mind — her heart yes, her heart, to a boy, to a man who loves her. But not like this. Not stolen from us like this.

ORFEO. She is expected to go. You understand that, Pilar? To the provinces. All girls, all patriots must go to teach —

PILAR. Patriots! Damn them to hell, the thieves who stole that word and turned it to filth.

ORFEO. She is expected to go to the provinces.

PILAR. I will never allow it.

ORFEO. It's only for three months. It will be good for her to get out of the city. Away from this madness. It's the perfect time.

PILAR. Why now? What has happened? What are you not telling me, Orfeo?

ORFEO. They came early in the morning. My students. With guns — do you see? To my lecture. Cellular division — do you know? They asked to address the hall — I said of course, and I offered them the lectern. They had orders for ten professors. But they wanted to assure the student body that Professor Santiago was on the list of the approved faculty. And they wanted the students to know that my classes would continue uninterrupted through this difficult period.

PILAR. I don't understand —

ORFEO. They took them away. Do you see? In chains.

PILAR. Why?

ORFEO. Don't be a fool, Pilar. They gave me a pin. And I put it on my lapel.

PILAR. Orfeo —

ORFEO. They'll come for me. Don't you see that? If we show any weakness, any sign of doubt, they'll come for me. They're already

56

watching me, reading my papers, reviewing my publications. We want to be careful. Marta — She talks too much. I think it might be best ...

PILAR. She has nowhere else to go.

ORFEO. We can hang a banner on the balcony.

PILAR. Stop it —

ORFEO. And Sonia —

PILAR. Please!

ORFEO. She has to go to teach — three months, no more. She has to go.

PILAR. Will you trade her flesh for your position?

ORFEO. To keep us safe? To see her marry? To hold my grandchildren? Oh yes, Pilar. I'll trade whatever I have. What God gave me, I'll trade for the chance — to live peacefully and die an old man, surrounded by my wife and daughter, and grandchildren. We can live — here — quietly. Stay here, live quietly. I'm not proud, Pilar, forgive me. I am not too proud. To keep her?

PILAR. To keep her. Yes. And if they say three more months, and another six cutting cane. And another year in the provinces, and another? How long will we stay quiet?

ORFEO. Not long. It won't be long, that's what I tell you. No one is going to sit back and watch us go the way of Moscow —

PILAR. You will.

ORFEO. Not so. Not so.

PILAR. We'll wait it out. We'll stay quiet. We'll cut cane. And you will stop your research, and I will trade kisses for luxuries. I can survive this. You can survive this. Of course we can. But not Sonia. Not her. It's our fault, Orfeo, because we loved her too well. Look at me, Orfeo. Look at me. It takes years to learn to be quiet. *(Orfeo looks away. Pilar goes on her knees to him.)* My darling. I beg you to listen. There is a way to get Sonia out — for a little while. You swear this madness won't last. I believe you. I do. But I am so afraid. I beg you to trust me now. Forgive me. I have done something — something —

ORFEO. What have you done, Pilar? *(Young Sonia enters, still wearing her uniform.)*

YOUNG SONIA. What are you whispering about? Why is everyone always whispering in this house?

PILAR. We thought you were sleeping.

YOUNG SONIA. I'm sorry I ran away at the rally, Papá. I know you must be upset about that. But I don't want any lecture from you.

ORFEO. I was worried about you.

YOUNG SONIA. Why? I'm not a china doll.

ORFEO. I know that.

YOUNG SONIA. They shot Professor Waldman.

PILAR. Oh my God.

ORFEO. I know.

YOUNG SONIA. Why?

ORFEO. I don't know.

YOUNG SONIA. He must have done something. He was teaching something? Was he smuggling? Sedition? He must have done something — what did he do?

PILAR. You mustn't look at your father like that.

YOUNG SONIA. You knew him — he was your colleague, what did he do?

ORFEO. I don't know. He told bad jokes. Made terrible coffee.

YOUNG SONIA. Papí? Are they coming for you?

ORFEO. Why would they? *(Beat.)*

YOUNG SONIA. I want to go to join the literacy campaign.

PILAR. No.

YOUNG SONIA. Tito goes to the provinces next week.

PILAR. My darling …

YOUNG SONIA. The schools are closed down. There is nothing for me to do, and we all have to help in this difficult time.

PILAR. Why go to the provinces? You can stay here and teach Marta.

YOUNG SONIA. I already talked to Tito about it, and he has signed me up.

ORFEO. Tito did this? Our Tito?

YOUNG SONIA. Yes. He is counting on me. It's only for the summer.

PILAR. The summer?

YOUNG SONIA. Yes. The summer! What's wrong with you? Tito! The summer! It's happening all over the place.

PILAR. Over my dead body. Over your father's dead body and mine.

YOUNG SONIA. You sound just like the nuns!

PILAR. That is not what you are here for.

YOUNG SONIA. What do you mean here? Do you mean on the planet?

PILAR. You know what I mean.

YOUNG SONIA. What am I on the planet for, Mamá? Can you tell me that? What have you done? I'm not going to end up like you, I know that much. I'm going to do something with my life. Things are changing everywhere, and I am part of it. And if I don't go this summer, I'll go next summer, or I'll just get out of the house soon and get married, and then I can do what I want. *(Pilar finds this incredibly funny.)* What? What?

PILAR. *(Laughing.)* Get married and do what you want? Oh mother of God.

YOUNG SONIA. Stop it! You always do that? What is it?

PILAR. Oh my dear, my dear one. *(She is erupting again, laughing.)*

ORFEO. Enough.

YOUNG SONIA. Fine. Don't tell me anything.

PILAR. I'm sorry. I am sorry. I'm sorry. We were only trying to give you some good news … Let me, Orfeo. *(Beat.)*

ORFEO. Yes. Tell her. Wonderful news, Sonia. Listen.

PILAR. Your father and I have found you a scholarship to attend school in the United States. They can take you right away.

YOUNG SONIA. I don't understand.

PILAR. *(To Orfeo.)* Study abroad.

ORFEO. *(To Pilar.)* For a year.

PILAR. *(To Orfeo.)* Anything you like. *(To Young Sonia.)* And then come back. You'll be sixteen by then. Old enough to make your own decisions. Go to the country. Or get married and ruin your own life. *(She starts laughing again.)* I'm sorry. Run your own life.

YOUNG SONIA. I can't go. I need —

PILAR. We have a visa.

YOUNG SONIA. How did you — the embassy is closed — how?

PILAR. A student visa. For students. For studying.

YOUNG SONIA. Papá?

ORFEO. My dove?

YOUNG SONIA. You're sending me away?

ORFEO. Never! This is to school. For a year.

YOUNG SONIA. But what about Tito — can I go in the fall?

PILAR. We've decided.

YOUNG SONIA. You haven't even talked to me — I won't go — You can't make me go.

MARTA. *(Entering from outside.)* It's madness out there — have you seen?

PILAR. What is it?

59

MARTA. The agency — there must have been a hundred people — I've never seen it like that — buying tickets —

YOUNG SONIA. Papá, look at me.

MARTA. They're going to realize something is going on — they're going to figure it out!

YOUNG SONIA. Why won't you look at me?

MARTA. Tito is standing outside. Watching. He saw me.

PILAR. Did you get a ticket?

YOUNG SONIA. Papí what is she talking about?

MARTA. I had to show them everything. The passport, the documents, I was trembling —

PILAR. Did he give you the ticket?

MARTA. It worked, it really worked.

PILAR. You got one?

MARTA. Yes. It's for tonight.

ORFEO. Tonight?

YOUNG SONIA. What?

ORFEO. Pilar?

MARTA. There were no other seats.

PILAR. Tonight —

MARTA. Everyone is talking about a secret invasion. How can there be secret invasion when everybody knows about it?

YOUNG SONIA. I don't understand.

PILAR. Your scholarship.

ORFEO. My darling. We have to get your things together. Warm clothes, Sonia. Would you like to see snow?

YOUNG SONIA. Why does Marta have my passport?

ORFEO. Ice crystals from the sky. No two are alike.

YOUNG SONIA. Answer me!

PILAR. We have a visa for you. But the ticket. To fly, you understand, my darling? The plane leaves tonight. You'll fly, Sonia. To America. And when things are normal again, when things are quiet — in the meantime, you'll study English there, and science.

YOUNG SONIA. Mamá. Please. I don't want to go. Please, don't make me. I don't have to go with Tito either. I can stay here. I can stay with you.

MARTA. Let me help you get your things together — Sonia, come with me — we don't have much time —

YOUNG SONIA. I can stay and teach Marta, I can help you here — (Knocking at the door.)

TITO. *(Offstage.)* Hello? Friends? I brought some posters by for you.
PILAR. Don't let him in.
ORFEO. Of course we have to —
YOUNG SONIA. Tito — come in — please come quickly — *(Opening the door.)*
TITO. Little one — what is all the fuss?
YOUNG SONIA. They're sending me away —
PILAR. Marta — get her a bag — pack a bag for her.
MARTA. This is a death sentence for us — do you understand that?
PILAR. On my mother's blood, Marta.
ORFEO. She can take a bag. One bag. *(Marta exits to the bedroom.)*
PILAR. Please, Tito, this is such a difficult time for us —
YOUNG SONIA. I don't want to go. Don't let them send me —
PILAR. She's won a scholarship. To study abroad. And now, silly thing, she doesn't want to go!
TITO. A scholarship! There seems to be an epidemic of scholarships going around. More contagious than the flu.
ORFEO. My friend —
TITO. I thought Sonia would be coming with us to the provinces for the summer.
YOUNG SONIA. I want to!
TITO. A difficult time to travel. Difficult to explain. And I've already promised the Ministry twenty teachers.
ORFEO. My old friend. This opportunity came so suddenly. We felt it was important to keep Sonia in school. But only for a month or two —
YOUNG SONIA. That's not what they said —
ORFEO. The opportunity — you understand?
YOUNG SONIA. They said a year!
TITO. All the same, difficult to explain, this. I've already promised twenty teachers. Twenty are expected, and if I only supply nineteen, it is my word on the line, you see.
PILAR. Take me.
YOUNG SONIA. Mamá!
ORFEO. My God, no —
PILAR. I want to go.
TITO. That would help my numbers.
PILAR. I want to serve my country. I am a patriot.
ORFEO. Dear God.

YOUNG SONIA. Mamá —

PILAR. I'll be ready to leave by the end of the week.

YOUNG SONIA. Don't take her. She's not strong. She faints, she's not strong. I can do the work. I'm ready.

TITO. My dear one, listen to your Uncle Tito. Listen to me, little one. Shh. No tears.

YOUNG SONIA. I can do the work.

TITO. Come here. *(He holds her gently in his arms.)* I tell you now, do as your parents wish. Do as they wish, as if it were the last thing they ever ask of you.

YOUNG SONIA. My home. My family —

TITO. Shh. Gentle. Your home. Our home, yes. You'll return to us. You'll return to us.

ORFEO. Sonia. It won't be for long.

YOUNG SONIA. Please don't send me away. Please, I beg you, I'll stay here. I'll stay home. I'll be quiet. Please, don't make me leave my home.

ORFEO. It's only for a little while. You can study there. For a little while.

YOUNG SONIA. You don't believe that.

MARTA. *(Entering from Sonia's room.)* Come pick out a dress to wear on the plane — come Sonia. Your prettiest one. *(Young Sonia and Marta exit.)*

TITO. Madam, please understand. I must deliver twenty teachers at the end of the week. Or it is my name that goes on the list.

PILAR. The list.

TITO. There is always a list. *(To Orfeo.)* A moment alone, my friend?

ORFEO. Help Sonia.

PILAR. What is it?

ORFEO. Go on, my dove. *(She exits.)*

TITO. Your posters.

ORFEO. I won't have them in my house. I'll burn them before I'll have them in my house.

TITO. Patience. A moment of madness.

ORFEO. I am out of patience.

TITO. Put up the posters, my friend. Put them up. I must tell you, there has been a report made, please there isn't time — a radio. It seems you have a radio —

ORFEO. This is not a crime.

TITO. It's nothing, a misunderstanding. It can be cleared up in a minute. Having a radio isn't a crime, you see. Not a crime. But the reception — unusual to receive broadcasts from so far. And to listen. Just give a simple explanation, when they come. The G-2 are very quick.

ORFEO. You reported us?

TITO. No. I knew, of course I knew. But I don't report everything. This came from another source. Another one. Overzealous, you see. But now, you see, the Ministry, they look at me and say —

ORFEO. I've done nothing wrong.

TITO. If you wanted to, quickly, perhaps, get some of your more precious things together, things, you understand, which could not be replaced if lost, I could, for a small fee, help them remain safe.

ORFEO. I am taking Sonia to the airport.

TITO. I'm sorry. I've been asked to detain you here for a time.

ORFEO. You want me to beg you, Tito. I will not. While I am gone, you can count the spoons. And the suits. Hang your posters. I am taking Sonia to the airport, and I will return because I am a man of my word. I will answer your questions, and I will go before your tribunal, and I will not give you a thing of myself. My soul goes on that plane with Sonia. Let me go, Tito.

TITO. I will do this for you.

YOUNG SONIA. *(Enters wearing a dress and heels with Marta.)* I have to say goodbye to my friends — *(Pilar follows with a half-full suitcase and a handful of clothes.)* I don't know what to pack. I don't have the right things.

ORFEO. Everything is all right now, Sonia. *(A nod from Tito.)* Everything — come — come — learn, watch everyone, study hard.

YOUNG SONIA. Why don't you come with me?

PILAR. *(Packing.)* You'll be home soon. Don't forget your home. Think about that. Think about flying over the island, can you imagine? Seeing the Sierra from the air, the curving golden coast, coral sands — The soaring towers of Havana —

YOUNG SONIA. I will go because you ask me. I go because I am a good daughter, and that's what you taught me to be. But never again. Let me be clear, Mamá, Papí, let me be so clear. After today, I am grown. And I am not yours anymore. Do you hear this? I am not yours anymore.

ORFEO. You mustn't say that.

PILAR. My heart.

YOUNG SONIA. No! No more. If I am old enough to be sent

away, then I am old enough to speak my mind to you. You can make me go and you can call it whatever you like. But I'm not yours anymore. I am not yours

PILAR. My heart, oh God, my heart.

YOUNG SONIA. I do not forgive you. I will never forgive you. *(She takes her bag and exits.)*

TITO. Words spoken in haste.

PILAR. She's right.

ORFEO. No.

PILAR. Promise me.

ORFEO. Anything.

PILAR. One year.

ORFEO. Yes.

PILAR. Or I will swim there myself.

ORFEO. Yes.

PILAR. I will swim there — *(Lights fade out. We hear the drone of airplanes overhead. Zak appears in his fatigues, as at the top of the act.)*

ZAK. My mother used to read me *Peter Pan*. The boy who could fly. He lived in Neverland with all the lost children. And one day, Peter got sad, and he missed home so much he flew back there — to the window of his bedroom. But his mother had locked it. And he couldn't get back in. I always used to wonder. Wouldn't you keep the window open. In case? Just in case? Wouldn't you? *(More planes are heard. Young Sonia walks through the* pecera *[literally translated, "the fishbowl"]: the airport hallway of glass that separates ticketed passengers from everyone else. Pilar and Orfeo call to her from the other side as she walks across the stage, not seeing them.)*

PILAR. Sonia!

ORFEO. Over here!

PILAR. One year —

ORFEO. We love you —

PILAR. She can't hear — whistle for her.

ORFEO. My darling, you'll be back soon.

PILAR. For your sixteenth birthday —

ORFEO. Look, we're here — look over here — don't forget — don't forget this!

PILAR. Whistle for her —

ORFEO. My mouth is dry. *(Young Sonia is gone. Orfeo and Pilar recede. Sonia appears as in Act One.)*

SONIA. I stood in the tiny bathroom in the airplane — five miles

64

over the sea — and out of my pocket, I pulled a handful of basil. And I threw it down the toilet. My ring. I took it off my finger, Spanish gold, from my great-grandmother's hand, passed down to me through a chain of pure love. And I flushed it away. And I said, "I do not forgive you. I will never forgive you. You have broken my heart."

None of us saw my father after that day. And my mother, true to her word. Walked into the sea. *(Pilar drowns in the waves. Transition lighting ...)*

Scene 5

2002. Arlington National Cemetery. Sonia, Jen and Daniel stand, heads bowed.

JEN. Mom?
SONIA. Mmm-hmm?
JEN. Grampa's in the car.
SONIA. Okay.
DANIEL. Go ahead. We'll be there in a minute.
JEN. Can I do anything?
SONIA. Go get warm, honey. *(Jen exits. Daniel and Sonia stand silent for a long time.)*
DANIEL. Honey?
SONIA. Another minute.
DANIEL. I love you.
SONIA. I love you.
DANIEL. I'll wait with Sam. *(It has begun to snow. Sonia stands alone, head bowed. She whispers the prayer very fast, an ancestral memory.)*
SONIA. *Dios te salve, María, llena eres de gracia, el Señor es contigo. Bendita tú eres entre todas las mujeres, y bendito es el fruto de tu vientre, Jesús. Santa María, Madre de Dios, ruega por nosotros pecadores, ahora y en la hora de nuestra muerte. Amén.* Forgive me. *(Zak enters in his dress military uniform. His uniform is pinned above his right elbow. He has lost the arm. They stand separated — do not embrace.)*

ZAK. Mom.

SONIA. Baby.

ZAK. Let's get you out of this weather.

SONIA. Tell me again.

ZAK. In the car.

SONIA. Please.

ZAK. Nina.

SONIA. Tell me about Nina.

ZAK. She loved dogs. Greyhounds.

SONIA. What else?

ZAK. She pulled me out of the truck. She was between me and the next blast. She ...

SONIA. You were afraid?

ZAK. I wasn't conscious.

SONIA. I wanted to thank her one last time.

ZAK. I'll thank her every day.

SONIA. To have another chance.

ZAK. Mom.

SONIA. Do you understand?

ZAK. I do.

SONIA. To have another chance with you.

ZAK. I know, Mom.

SONIA. I want to tell you what happened. In Cuba. In my mind, I've told you a million times. I loved them so much, my family — I wonder all the time if I could have — if I had stayed —

ZAK. I'm here. Because of you.

SONIA. I didn't keep you safe.

ZAK. It was the right thing, Mom. The right thing for me.

SONIA. Yes

ZAK. No regrets.

SONIA. I have so many.

ZAK. Let's go, Mom. Take me there. Could you take me? Show me the beaches. The buildings. Those old cars.

SONIA. We'd have to fly.

ZAK. No. We could — couldn't we take a boat?

SONIA. A boat? *(They stand gazing at each other as the lights fade out.)*

End of Play

PROPERTY LIST

Tableware
Jell-O molds
Keys, wallet
"Thingy"
Luggage
Pastry box with string
Wine, glasses
Candlesticks, candles, matches
Food
Milk carton
Coffee, cup
Juice carton
Coat
Pastry boxes
Cuban big-print newspaper
Red kerchief
Glasses, rum, tray
Small box with star pin
Basil leaves
Socks
Ice, yellow towel
Banners
Cuban passport
Suitcase, clothes

SOUND EFFECTS

Waves
Motor
Engine sounds
Gunfire
Explosions
Cuban radio, music, speeches
Radio Swan
Radio scanning, then music
Rally noise, shouting
Airplane drone

NEW PLAYS

★ **AT HOME AT THE ZOO by Edward Albee.** Edward Albee delves deeper into his play THE ZOO STORY by adding a first act, HOMELIFE, which precedes Peter's fateful meeting with Jerry on a park bench in Central Park. "An essential and heartening experience." *–NY Times.* "Darkly comic and thrilling." *–Time Out.* "Genuinely fascinating." *–Journal News.* [2M, 1W] ISBN: 978-0-8222-2317-7

★ **PASSING STRANGE book and lyrics by Stew, music by Stew and Heidi Rodewald, created in collaboration with Annie Dorsen.** A daring musical about a young bohemian that takes you from black middle-class America to Amsterdam, Berlin and beyond on a journey towards personal and artistic authenticity. "Fresh, exuberant, bracingly inventive, bitingly funny, and full of heart." *–NY Times.* "The freshest musical in town!" *–Wall Street Journal.* "Excellent songs and a vulnerable heart." *–Variety.* [4M, 3W] ISBN: 978-0-8222-2400-6

★ **REASONS TO BE PRETTY by Neil LaBute.** Greg really, truly adores his girlfriend, Steph. Unfortunately, he also thinks she has a few physical imperfections, and when he mentions them, all hell breaks loose. "Tight, tense and emotionally true." *–Time Magazine.* "Lively and compulsively watchable." *–The Record.* [2M, 2W] ISBN: 978-0-8222-2394-8

★ **OPUS by Michael Hollinger.** With only a few days to rehearse a grueling Beethoven masterpiece, a world-class string quartet struggles to prepare their highest-profile performance ever—a televised ceremony at the White House. "Intimate, intense and profoundly moving." *–Time Out.* "Worthy of scores of bravissimos." *–BroadwayWorld.com.* [4M, 1W] ISBN: 978-0-8222-2363-4

★ **BECKY SHAW by Gina Gionfriddo.** When an evening calculated to bring happiness takes a dark turn, crisis and comedy ensue in this wickedly funny play that asks what we owe the people we love and the strangers who land on our doorstep. "As engrossing as it is ferociously funny." *–NY Times.* "Gionfriddo is some kind of genius." *–Variety.* [2M, 3W] ISBN: 978-0-8222-2402-0

★ **KICKING A DEAD HORSE by Sam Shepard.** Hobart Struther's horse has just dropped dead. In an eighty-minute monologue, he discusses what path brought him here in the first place, the fate of his marriage, his career, politics and eventually the nature of the universe. "Deeply instinctual and intuitive." *–NY Times.* "The brilliance is in the infinite reverberations Shepard extracts from his simple metaphor." *–TheaterMania.* [1M, 1W] ISBN: 978-0-8222-2336-8

DRAMATISTS PLAY SERVICE, INC.
440 Park Avenue South, New York, NY 10016 212-683-8960 Fax 212-213-1539
postmaster@dramatists.com   www.dramatists.com

NEW PLAYS

★ **AUGUST: OSAGE COUNTY by Tracy Letts.** WINNER OF THE 2008 PULITZER PRIZE AND TONY AWARD. When the large Weston family reunites after Dad disappears, their Oklahoma homestead explodes in a maelstrom of repressed truths and unsettling secrets. "Fiercely funny and bitingly sad." *–NY Times.* "Ferociously entertaining." *–Variety.* "A hugely ambitious, highly combustible saga." *–NY Daily News.* [6M, 7W] ISBN: 978-0-8222-2300-9

★ **RUINED by Lynn Nottage.** WINNER OF THE 2009 PULITZER PRIZE. Set in a small mining town in Democratic Republic of Congo, RUINED is a haunting, probing work about the resilience of the human spirit during times of war. "A full-immersion drama of shocking complexity and moral ambiguity." *–Variety.* "Sincere, passionate, courageous." *–Chicago Tribune.* [8M, 4W] ISBN: 978-0-8222-2390-0

★ **GOD OF CARNAGE by Yasmina Reza, translated by Christopher Hampton.** WINNER OF THE 2009 TONY AWARD. A playground altercation between boys brings together their Brooklyn parents, leaving the couples in tatters as the rum flows and tensions explode. "Satisfyingly primitive entertainment." *–NY Times.* "Elegant, acerbic, entertainingly fueled on pure bile." *–Variety.* [2M, 2W] ISBN: 978-0-8222-2399-3

★ **THE SEAFARER by Conor McPherson.** Sharky has returned to Dublin to look after his irascible, aging brother. Old drinking buddies Ivan and Nicky are holed up at the house too, hoping to play some cards. But with the arrival of a stranger from the distant past, the stakes are raised ever higher. "Dark and enthralling Christmas fable." *–NY Times.* "A timeless classic." *–Hollywood Reporter.* [5M] ISBN: 978-0-8222-2284-2

★ **THE NEW CENTURY by Paul Rudnick.** When the playwright is Paul Rudnick, expectations are geared for a play both hilarious and smart, and this provocative and outrageous comedy is no exception. "The one-liners fly like rockets." *–NY Times.* "The funniest playwright around." *–Journal News.* [2M, 3W] ISBN: 978-0-8222-2315-3

★ **SHIPWRECKED! AN ENTERTAINMENT—THE AMAZING ADVENTURES OF LOUIS DE ROUGEMONT (AS TOLD BY HIMSELF) by Donald Margulies.** The amazing story of bravery, survival and celebrity that left nineteenth-century England spellbound. Dare to be whisked away. "A deft, literate narrative." *–LA Times.* "Springs to life like a theatrical pop-up book." *–NY Times.* [2M, 1W] ISBN: 978-0-8222-2341-2

DRAMATISTS PLAY SERVICE, INC.
440 Park Avenue South, New York, NY 10016 212-683-8960 Fax 212-213-1539
postmaster@dramatists.com www.dramatists.com